TRADITIONAL QUILTS II
The *Easy* Way
by Sharon Hultgren

95 Mayhill Street
Saddle Brook, NJ 07662

This book is dedicated to my mother. She has shown such courage, strength and faith. I hope that if I am ever put to the test, I can be the woman she has shown herself to be. What a lady! I love you mom.

Acknowledgements:

©1992. Sharon Hultgren. No portion of this book may be reproduced by any means without written permission of the author. She may be contacted through the publisher.

Published by EZ International, 95 Mayhill Street, Saddle Brook, NJ 07662.

Graphic design and layout: Shimp Personalized Publication Services, Inc., Las Vegas, NV.

Photography: Joel Butkowski Photographers, St. Cloud, MN.

Printed in Hong Kong

ISBN: 1-881588-25-4.

Table of Contents

Introduction 4

Tool Tutorial and Construction Tips 5
    Using Easy Angle™ 7
    Using Easy Angle II™ 8
    Using Easy Six™ 9
    Using Easy Eight™ 10
    Using Easy Hexagon™ 11
    Using Companion Angle™ 12
    Secrets for Successful Setting In 14
    A Bit About Borders 15

Projects 17
    Appliqué Heart Template 18
    Cabin in the Woods 19
    Winter Pines Table Cover 22
    Ohio Star 23
    Happy-Go-Round 25
    One Sunday Morning 39
    Wedding Ring 40
    Inner City, the Easy Way 42
    Take Your Stand, Yes, Ma'm! 44
    Grandmother's Flower Garden 46
    Stars All Around 48
    Windy Hill 50
    From My Attic Window 52
    Spinning Spools 54
    Jacob's Ladder 56
    Nora's Star 58
    Paducah 60

Coloring Blocks 62

Photographs 27-38

Introduction

This book is a combination of old and new, which is the way life is supposed to be. There are quilts found while I was traveling, quilts made because of a special memory, quilts made by accident and some by fleeting inspiration. We all wish the old quilts could tell their story. Where were the fabrics worn before they found their way to the quilt top? What would the makers of some of these quilts say if they knew their quilt top was finished and even published?

It is my hope that as you make some of the quilts found in this book that you will catch the excitement of being part of the ongoing history of quiltmaking.

Sharon Hultgren

Tool Tutorial

and a few Construction Tips

Using Easy Angle™

Easy Angle™ provides a quick method to cut right triangles. Just add seam allowance to your finished size, place two cut strips of fabric right sides together, then counter-cut with the Easy Angle™. The lines on the tool are provided at ¼" increments, and are used for aligning fabric strips for cutting. The heavier lines are provided at ½" increments.

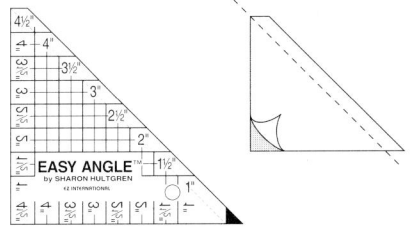

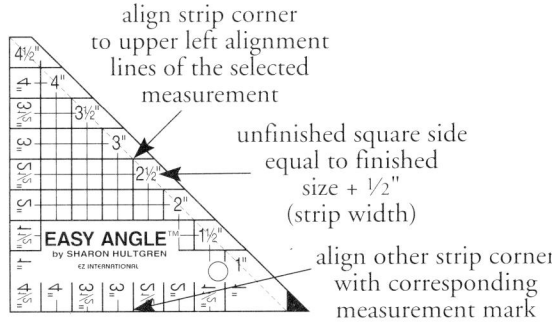

Use of the tool requires that you select a finished square size. Once you do this, add ½" to get the corresponding unfinished triangle size. Find the unfinished size on the tool and the alignment lines above and to the left of this number.

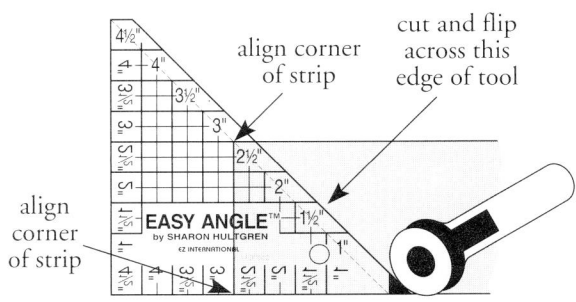

Cut strips equal to the unfinished width of the triangle size. Lay the strips right sides together. Align the bottom of the tool on the bottom edge of the strip. Slide the tool to the right until the correct number is in the upper left corner of the fabric. The entire number must be on the fabric. Cut along the diagonal edge of the tool.

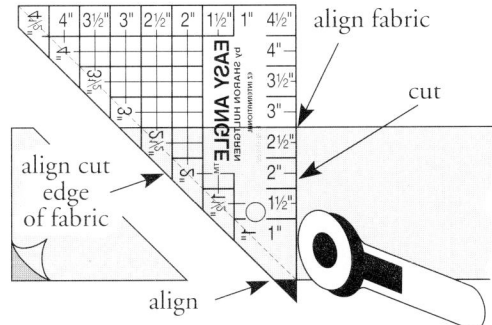

Flip the tool over on the diagonal edge and align the tool so that the cut edge of the fabric aligns with the tool and the bottom edge of the fabric aligns with the top of the black triangle on the tool. Cut along the perpendicular edge of the tool. Repeat these last two steps until you have cut all of your triangles. You will have pairs of triangles which you may string through your machine to make the triangle-squares. Note that the pieces for the square are already right sides together.

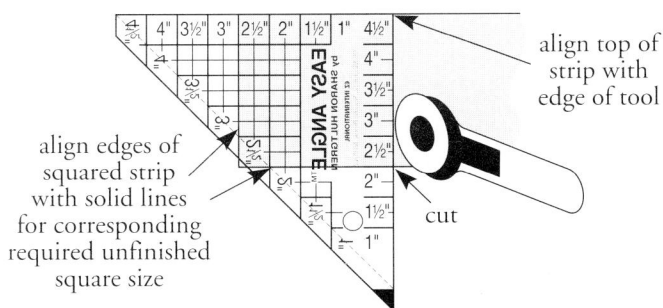

To make single fabric squares up to 4½", cut a strip equal to the unfinished square size. Align the tool with the top edge of the strip and slide it along the strip until the left side of the strip aligns with the vertical line on the tool representing the unfinished square size.

Using Easy Angle II™

Easy Angle II™ has all the capabilities of the original Easy Angle™ but with a range of 3"-10½". The lines on the tool are provided at ¼" increments, and are used for aligning fabric strips for cutting. The heavier lines are provided at ½" increments. Also included are ¼" seam allowances.

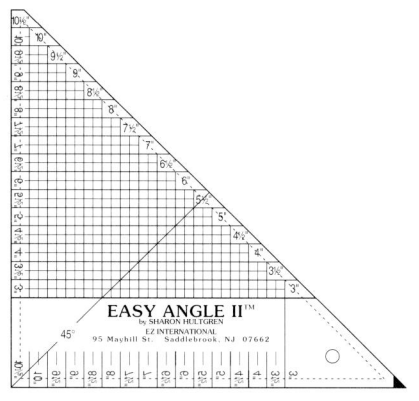

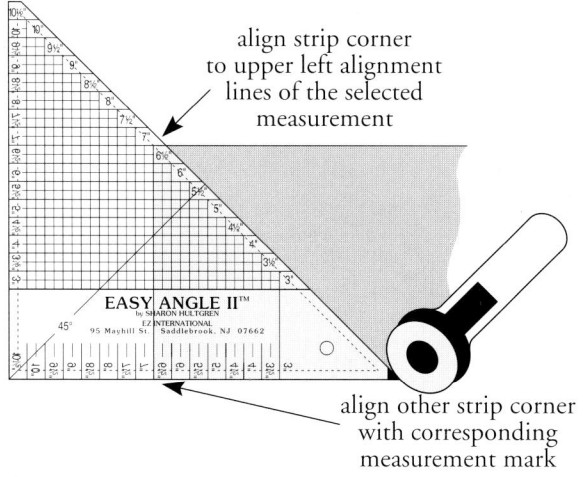

Cut strips equal to the unfinished width of the triangle size. Lay the strips right sides together. Align the bottom of the tool on the bottom edge of the strip. Slide the tool to the right until the correct number is in the upper left corner of the fabric. The entire number must be on the fabric. Cut along the diagonal edge of the tool.

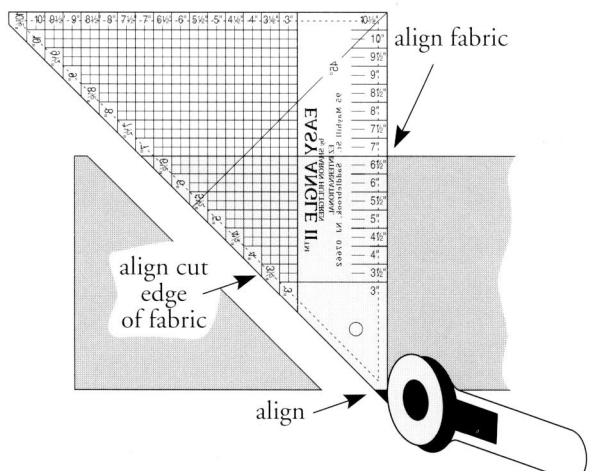

Flip the tool over on the diagonal edge and align the tool so that the cut edge of the fabric aligns with the tool and the bottom edge of the fabric aligns with the top of the black triangle on the tool. Cut along the perpendicular edge of the tool. Repeat these last two steps until you have cut all of your triangles. You will have pairs of triangles which you may string through your machine to make the triangle-squares. Note that the pieces for the square are already right sides together.

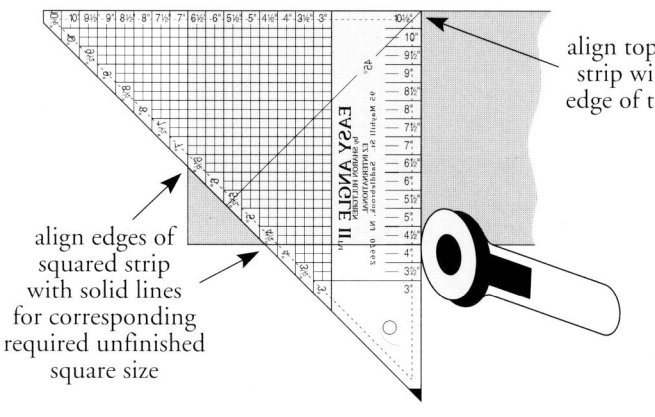

To make single fabric squares up to 10½", cut a strip equal to the unfinished square size. Align the tool with the top edge of the strip and slide it along the strip until the left side of the strip aligns with the vertical line on the tool representing the unfinished square size.

Using Easy Six™

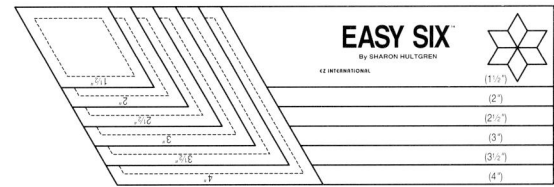

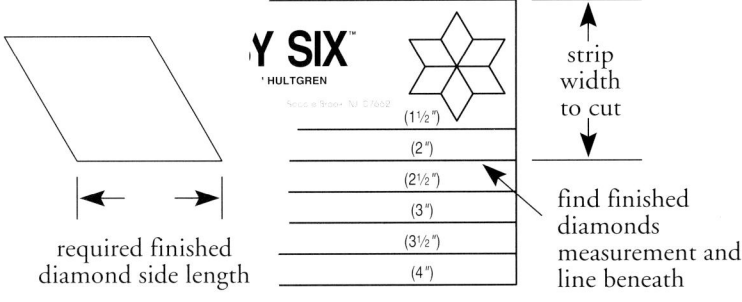

The Easy Six™ tool is designed to make quick and accurate six pointed stars and tumbling blocks. The star points can have finished edges of 2", 2½", 3", 3½", and 4".

Fold the fabric once with the selvege edges together and then fold again bringing the fold to the selveges. The Easy Six™ will now be wider than the fabric.

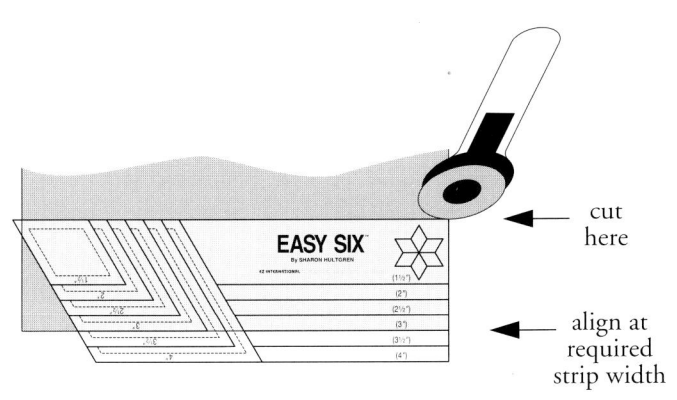

Select the size of star points desired. Hold the tool so that you can read the tool name and the straight edge bold lines are on the right end of the tool. Place the bottom edge of the fabric on the line that notes the desired size of the star point you want. In the example, we have selected a 3" point. Cut along the top edge of the fabric. Please note that the strip will not measure 3" wide.

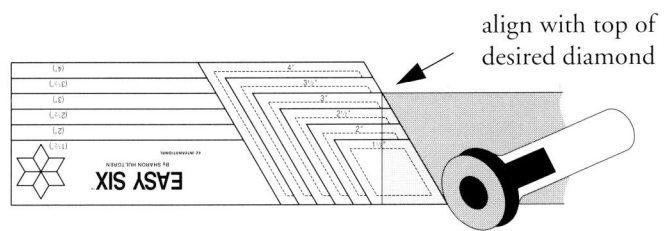

Rotate the tool as shown, so that the points are on you right. Line the bottom edge of the tool with the bottom edge of the fabric strip. Slide the tool to the left so that you can cut the angle.

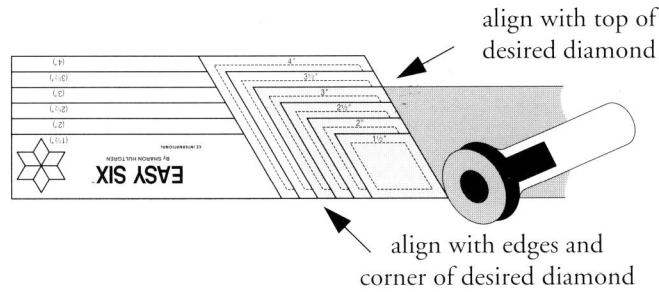

Keeping the bottom edge of the tool lined up with the bottom edge of the fabric, slide the Easy Six™ to the right until the fabric fills the desired point and then cut along the diagonal edge of the tool. Continue to slide the tool to the right and cut as many points as needed. Several layers can be cut at one time.

Using Easy Eight™

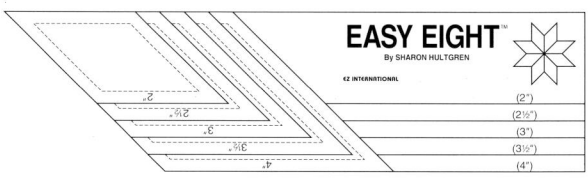

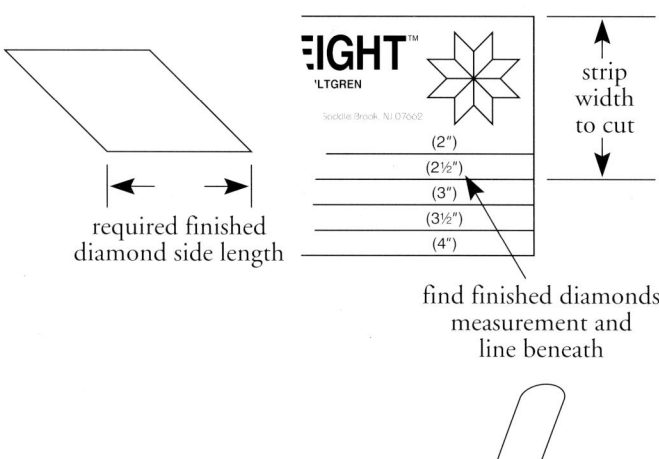

Easy Eight™ makes it easy to do the eight-pointed stars you will find in several of the projects. It allows for five sizes of diamonds, as indicated on the tool.

This tool is very easy to use. First determine the length of the side of your finished diamond. Then find that number on the tool, and the corresponding line underneath. The 2½" size is chosen as an example.

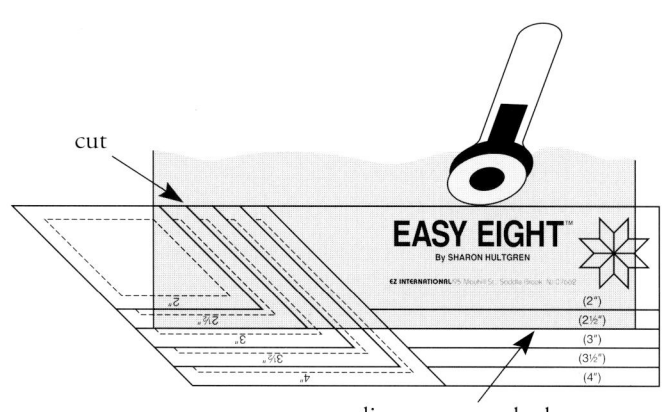

Fold your fabric and square up one end perpendicular to the folds. Lay the tool over the edge and line up the edge with the line underneath the finished diamond size number. Then cut strips. Note that the width of the strip will not be the same as the alignment number on the tool. The number represents the diamond size and the line underneath gives the strip width.

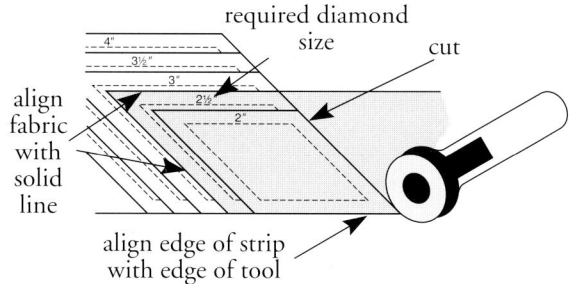

When cutting the diamonds from the strip, turn the tool around and line up the strip with the tool as indicated. Cut the triangle off of the corner.

Slide the tool along the strip until the edge of the strip aligns with the solid line representing the outline of the unfinished diamond for the diamond size. Cut the diamond from the strip. Repeat this step for additional diamonds. Repeat these last two steps for each strip.

Using Easy Hexagon™

The Easy Hexagon™ is designed so that you can cut the strip and the hexagon shape with a rotary cutter. The hexagons are given in five different sizes and the length of the finished edge is given. Fabric should be folded once with the selvege edges together and then folded again bringing the fold to the selveges. Now select the size hexagon you want to use.

Set the straightened bottom edge of the fabric on the bold line that indicates the size you have chosen. Cut along the top edge of the Easy Hexagon™. (See top graphic to the left.)

Rotate the Easy Hexagon™ so that the hexagon shapes are on the right hand side of this tool.

Line the bottom edge of the fabric strip on the bottom edge of the Easy Hexagon™. Note that the bold 2" line is now on the top edge of the fabric.

Open the fabric strip so the fabric is only folded once. Place the selvege edge on the left. Slide the Easy Hexagon™ to the left.

Cut along the Easy Hexagon™ as shown.

Turn diamond shapes.

Set diamond shape under the Easy Hexagon™ and trim the small triangles.

Hexagons are now ready for piecing.

Using Companion Angle™

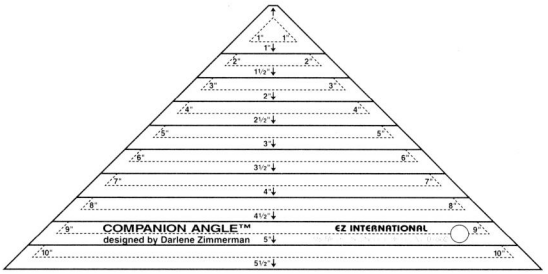

Use Companion Angle™ to make triangles with the long edge on the outside of a block, border, or quilt. Cut the triangles with the long edge on the straight of the grain.

Dashed lines represent sewing lines and show the **finished** triangle size, based on a ¼" seam allowance; center numbers represent the width of the strip to cut; solid lines underneath are used for alignment (for example, cut a 2½" strip for **finished** 4" triangles.)

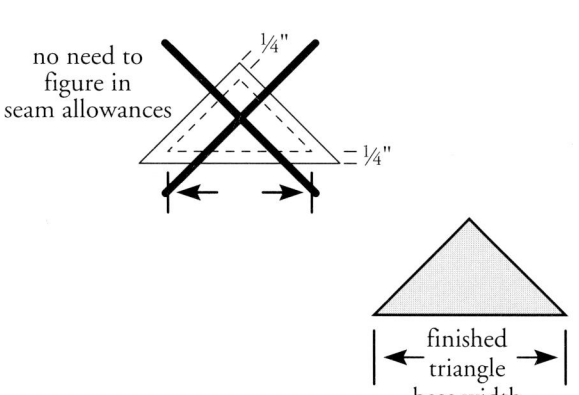

Determine the required size of the long edge of your finished triangle.

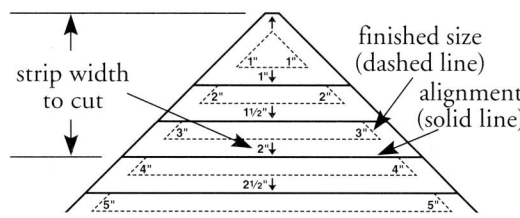

Determine the required strip width to cut to get the desired triangle size.

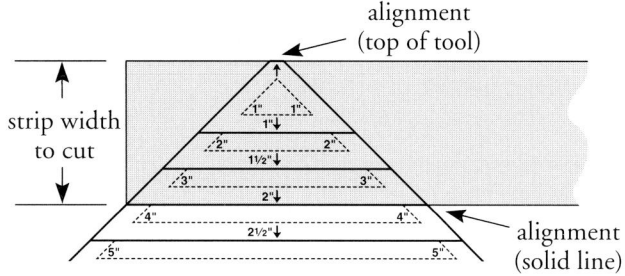

Align the tool edge with the edge of the strip.

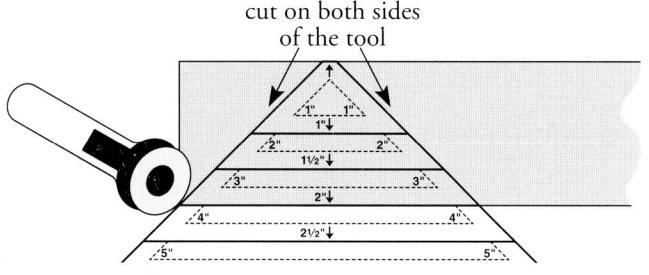

Cut on both sides of the tool.

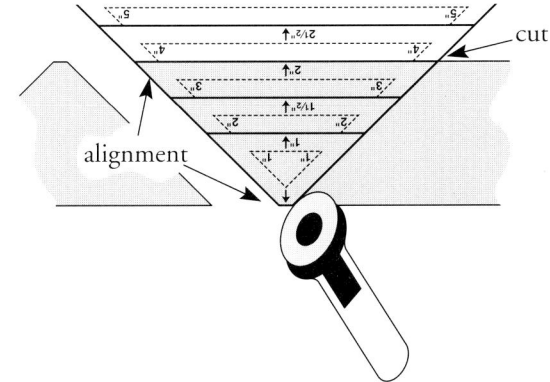

Invert the tool and cut another triangle; continue in this manner across the strip of fabric.

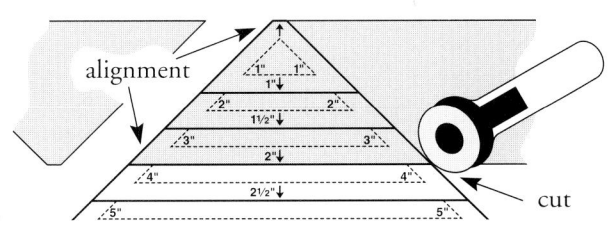

As you continue across the strip, make sure that the top of the tool, the alignment line you are using, and the edge of the triangle are positioned correctly.

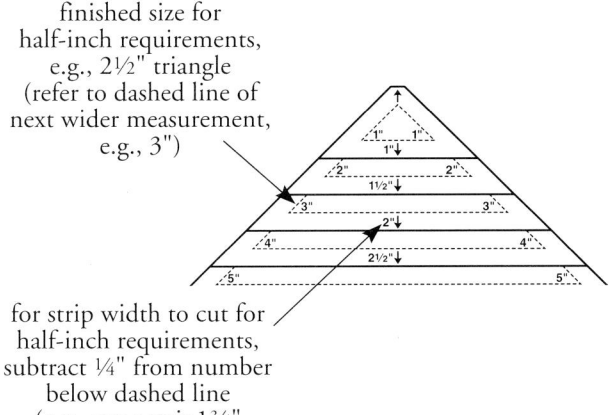

finished size for half-inch requirements, e.g., 2½" triangle (refer to dashed line of next wider measurement, e.g., 3")

for strip width to cut for half-inch requirements, subtract ¼" from number below dashed line (e.g., cut a strip 1¾" for a 2½" finished triangle)

You can use this tool to cut triangles that have other than whole inch long edges. The role of the dashed and solid lines are reversed. Align on dashed line.

Companion Tools

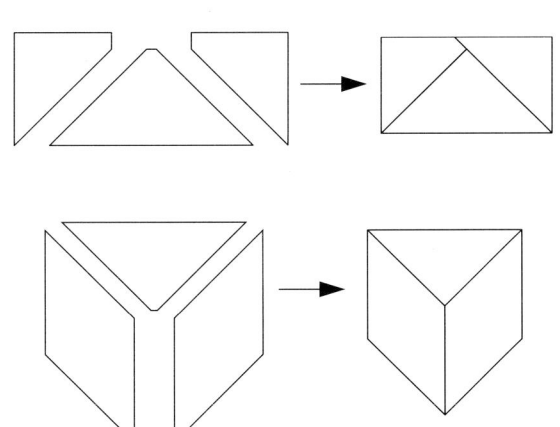

The Easy Angle™ and Companion Angle™ tools create pieces which fit together perfectly when cut from the same width strips. Now Flying Geese are a snap.

The Easy Eight™ and Companion Angle™ tools are also perfectly matched, when pieces are cut from strips measured with the Easy Eight™ tool. Matching pieces for setting in the eight pointed star has never been easier.

Secrets for Successful Setting In

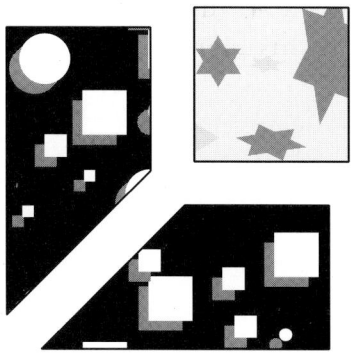

There are many patterns in quilting that must be completed by "setting in." Examples are: Eight-pointed Stars, Grandmothers Flower Garden, Attic Windows, etc. This is a process feared by many quilters. If you follow a few simple steps, it is really very easy.

When stitching, begin from the outside and stitch toward the inside. This will eliminate any tendency of one piece being longer than the other on the outside edge when the stitching is complete. When coming to the inside seam intersection, STOP! Do not stitch over the seam allowance or beyond the seam intersection. Pull the piece that you are sewing away from the sewing machine.

Cut the threads at least 1½" long. Yes, you will have threads inside the quilt. If they are cut short, the seam could open up. It is better to take one stitch too many, and gently pull it out, than to be a stitch short. It is possible to sew in reverse when you come to the seam intersection, but do this only if you really know your sewing machine.

To set in the piece, first lay the piece right sides together on one of the framing pieces and sew from the outside in. Next, open the piece just sewn in and fold the third piece over it. Sew this seam from the outside edge in, also.

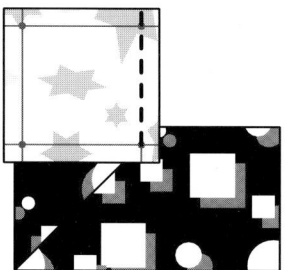

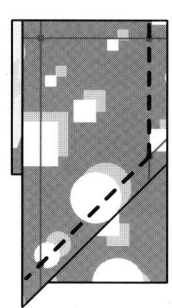

The final trick is to finger press the seams in the direction they should go and then press the piece on the right side with a hot, dry iron. Steam will distort the shape of the piece. Remember, the direction that you press the seam allowance will cause that area to be raised above the other. Also, remember the motto, "Perfect piecing is a pressing matter!"

A Bit About Borders

Borders put the finishing touch on your quilt. They can be very simple or very ornate. The fabric should be the same that is seen in the quilt body. A thin accent color, like a matting on a picture, can really set the quilt, but the other color(s) should be the same. The opposite borders should be equal in length. If you are short of fabric or just because it looks nice it is also possible to put a contrast or pieced block in the corner. It must be the same size as the border.

Take a measurement 12" in from the edge of your quilt. The border length should be the average of the numbers from the two sides. The length (or width) of border pieces will be the average of the two measurements in that direction. I.e., the width of the top border piece will be

$$\frac{W_1 + W_2}{2}$$

Mitered corners for adjacent pieces of a round of borders are made after the pieces are attached to the quilt top. First, attach the adjacent border pieces, sewing to within one seam allowance of either corner of the quilt top. Next, fold the quilt top right sides together on a 45° angle from the corner to be mitered. The corner pieces now are also right sides together. Then align the Easy Angle II™ ¼" dashed line with the quilt top fold line and trim the border pieces along the long edge of the tool.

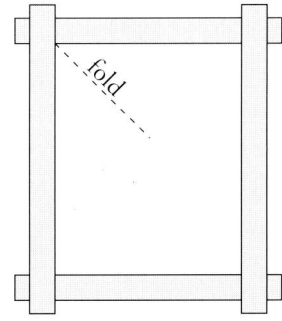

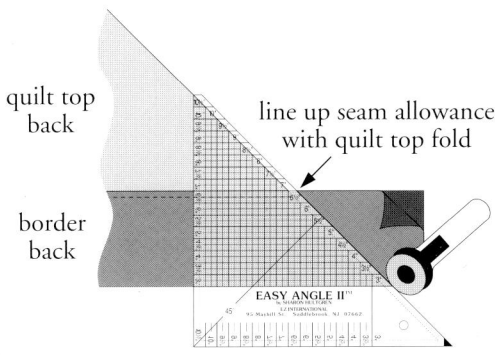

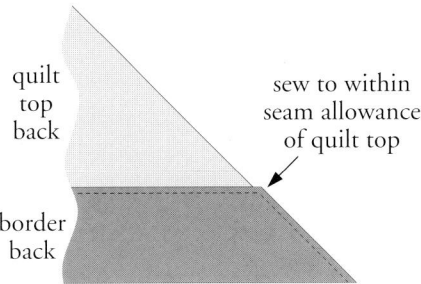

Sew from the outside to the seam allowance intersection.

Do this for each corner of the quilt.

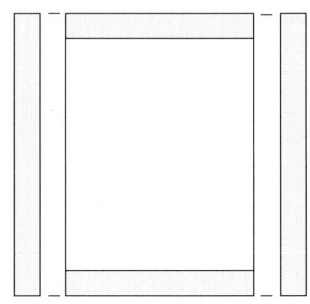

Box borders are the easiest to make. Add the top and bottom borders first, measure the new length of the quilt, and add the side borders.

Projects

Appliqué template for Table Cover. Directions begin on page 19.

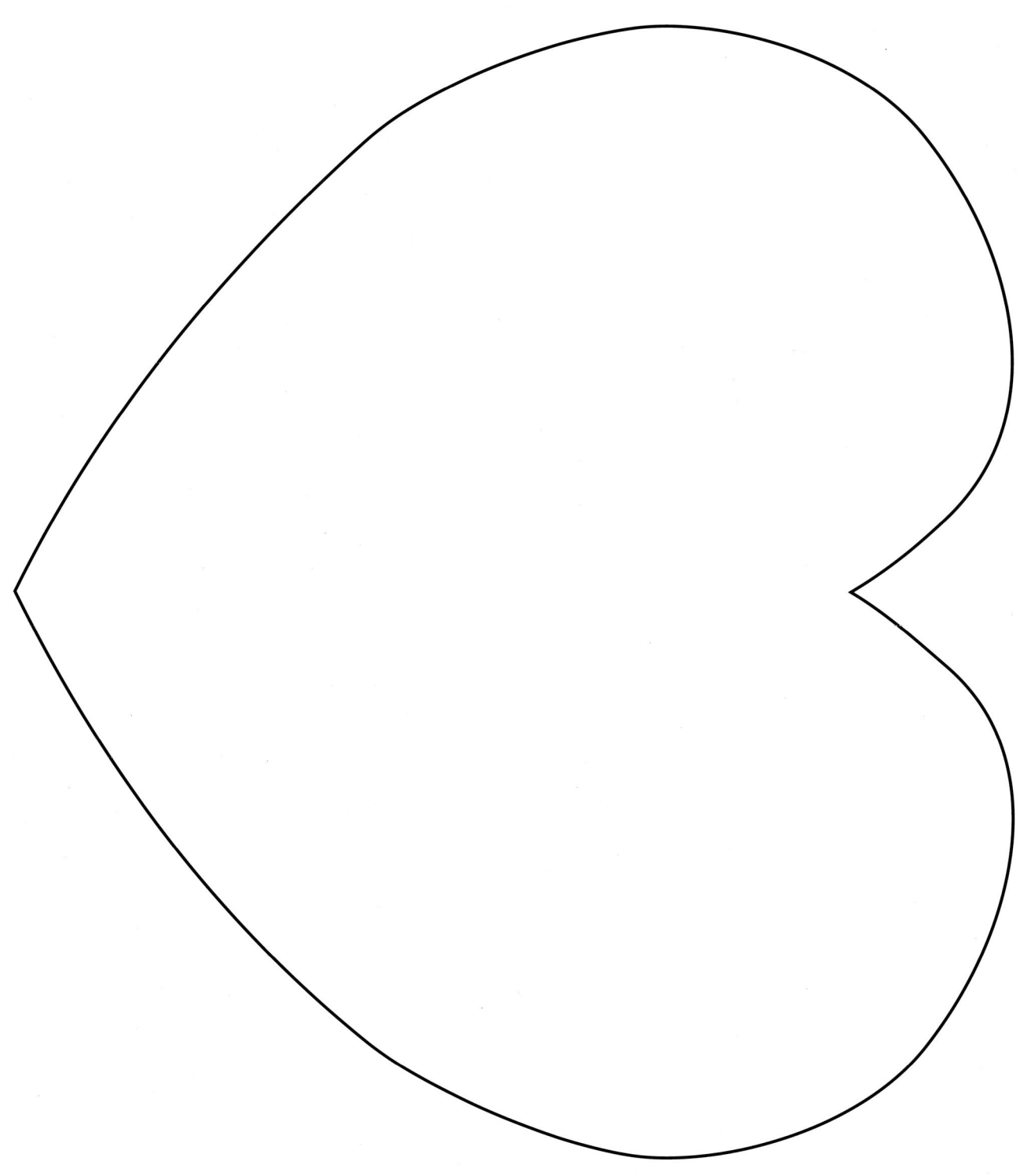

Cabin in the Woods
59" x 74"
See photo on page 29.

This warm fireside quilt is just waiting for someone to light the fire and find a friend or book, furry or otherwise. The blocks can be arranged in any order. When my son was in the Sinai Desert as part of a Multi-national Peace Keeping Force, I sent him a smaller version of this quilt. I felt it would bring a touch of the North Woods that he loves to his office in the desert.

Fabric Requirements: 59" x 74"

Background	¾ yard
Trees	¾ yard
Plaid sashing	1¼ yards
Red sashing & border	2 yards
Tan squares	¾ yard
Green border	½ yard
Roof	¼ yard
House	¼ yard
Binding, your choice	¾ yard

Tools Needed: Easy Angle™ • Easy Angle II™ • Companion Angle™

Cabin Square Construction

Cutting Requirements:

Background	1 - 4½" strip
	2 - 1½" strips
House	1 - 6½" strip
Roof	1 - 4½" strip

Sew the 1½" background strips to each side of the house strip. Press the seam allowance toward the house. Cut this piece into 4½" bars as shown here.

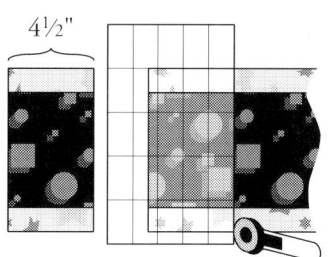

Using the Easy Angle™ cut the 4½" strip of background fabric into triangles. Using the Companion Angle™ cut the 4½" strip of roof fabric into triangles.

Sew the background triangles onto either side of the roof. Press the seam toward the roof. Sew the top half and the bottom half of the block together. Press the seam allowance toward the roof. You will be able to make seven complete cabin blocks.

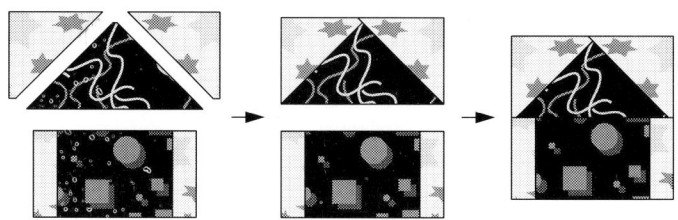

Pine Tree Construction

Cutting Requirements:	
Background	1 - 2½" strip
Tree	1 - 2½" strip

This block is made with a left and a right side. The pieces are cut from strips that are cut 2½" wide. Each color must be cut separately with right sides together. This will cause the pieces to have a right side and a left side.

Set the tree out the way it should be sewn. Sew the background to the tree branch first. Press the seam allowance toward the tree. Sew the rows together. Press the seams up. Sew the center seam. Press this seam open.

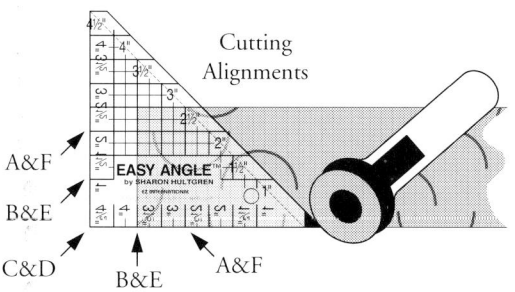

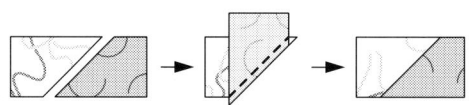

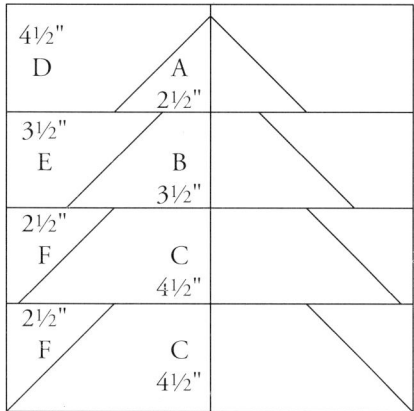

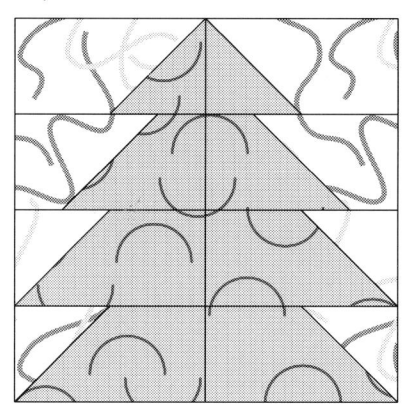

Sashing Construction

Cutting Requirements:	
Sashing	4 - 8½" strips
Counter-cut	32 - 2½" pieces
Tan	4 - 2½" strips
Red	18 - 1½" strips
Counter-cut	16 - 12½" pieces

After you counter-cut two of the 8½" strips into thirty-two 2½" pieces,

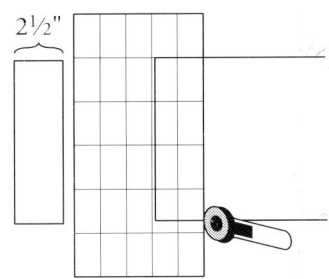

then sew these to each side of the cabin and pine tree blocks.

 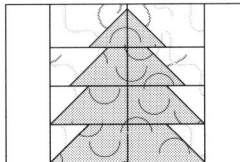

Next sew the 2½" wide tan strips to the long sides of the remaining 8½" wide sashing strips. Counter-cut into 30 - 2½" strips.

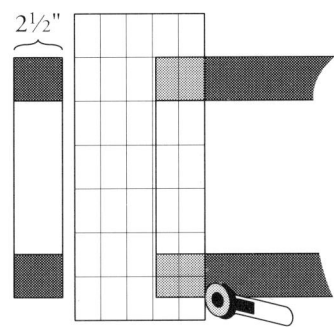

Sew these to the top and bottom of each cabin and pine tree block. There will be some extra strips which will be sewn around the edge of the quilt after the blocks are put together.

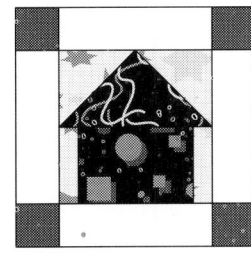 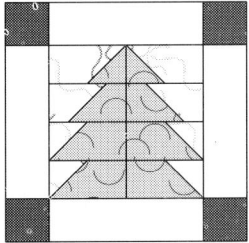

Sew the red strips between the blocks as connectors. After the blocks are sewn side by side, join the rows with the remaining red strips. Join the red strips end to end when needed for the length. Add bars and squares to the edges after the blocks are joined.

Borders

Cutting Requirements:	
Green	6 - 2" strips
Red	6 - 6½" strips

Join these together short end to short end as needed and sew to the outside edges of the quilt. Follow the guidelines in the section on *Borders*, page 15 for complete details.

Yardages are provided here for a larger quilt.

Fabric Requirements: 81" x 94" (5 blocks x 6 blocks)	
Background	1¼ yards
Trees	1¼ yards
Plaid sashing	2½ yards
Red sashing & border	3½ yards
Tan squares	1¼ yards
Green border	¾ yard
Roof	½ yard
House	½ yard
Binding, your choice	1 yard

Winter Pines Table Cover
60" across
See photo on page 28.

First make the pine tree squares. Follow the directions given on page 20. Cut three 8½" strips, then counter-cut eight sets of 10½" and eight sets of 3½". Sew to the top (A) and bottom (B) of the tree. (See figure to the right.)

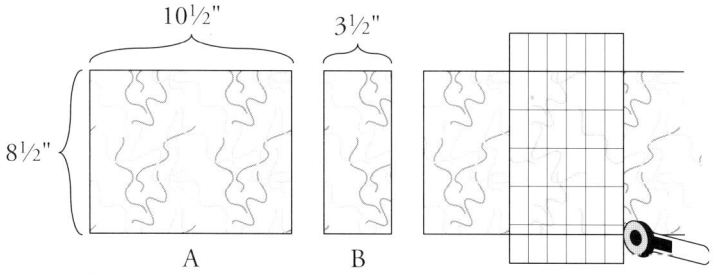

To make background triangles, cut two pieces 20" x 42". Mark both edges carefully as shown. Cut on drawn lines. Sew these to the sides of the Pine sections. The hearts are then machine appliquéd onto this wedge. The appliqué heart can be found on page 19.

Make eight sections as shown below, then sew together forming a circle.

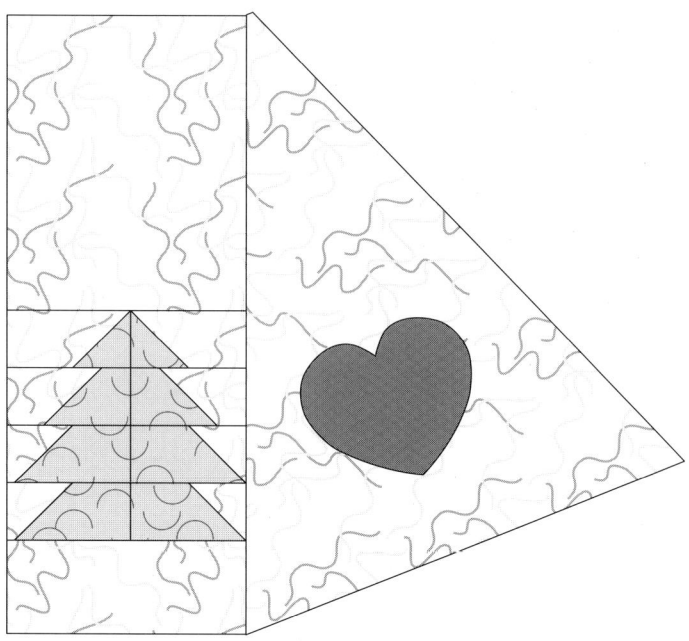

Cut a 20" square for the center section and trim the corners off as shown below. Set in, stitching from seam intersection to seam intersection.

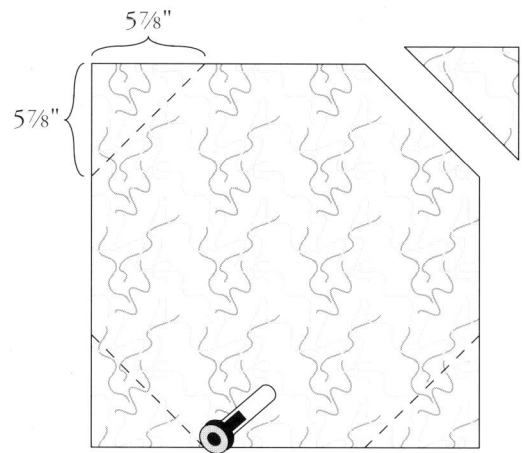

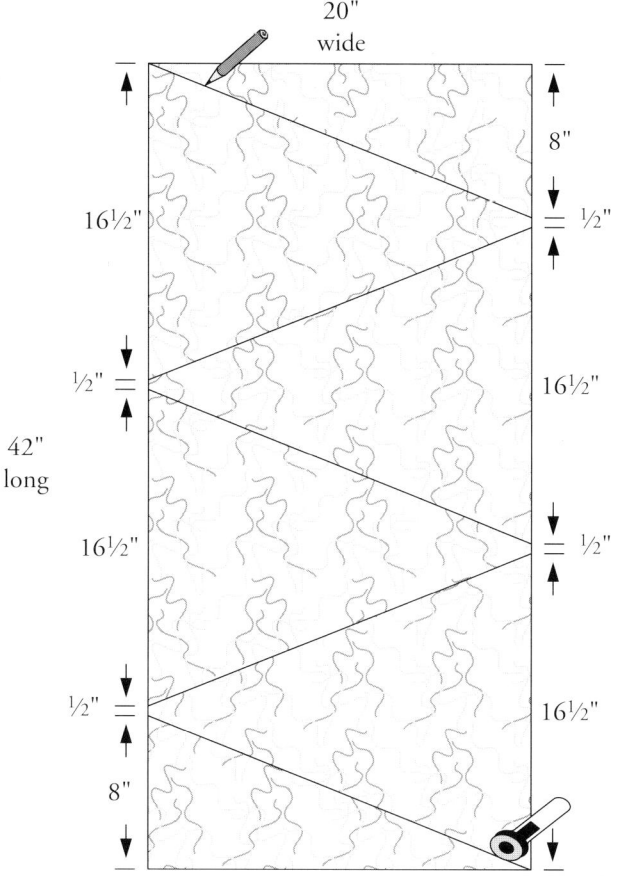

Fabric Requirements:

Background	3 yards
A & B (same fabric)	¾ yard
Green	¾ yard
Trees (background)	½ yard

Ohio Star

See photo on page 36.

Ohio Star is deceptively easy to make! Carefully sew with ¼" seams and match the seam intersections and you won't have any trouble. The beauty of a two color quilt is especially nice in this quilt.

Tools Needed:
Easy Angle™ • Companion Angle™

	Fabric Requirements:		
	Crib 44" x 44" 5 pieced blocks 4 plain blocks 3 x 3	Fireside 66" x 66" 13 pieced blocks 12 plain blocks 5 x 5	Full/Queen 88" x 108" 32 pieced blocks 31 plain blocks 7 x 9
White	1 yard	2½ yards	6 yards
Gold	2 yards	3 yards	5 yards
Strips to Cut: Blocks			
White	5 - 3"	13 - 3"	32 - 3"
Gold	3 - 3"	7 - 3"	16 - 3"
Gold	1 - 4"	2 - 4"	4 - 4"
White	1 - 10½"	3 - 10½"	8 - 10½"
Strips to Cut: Borders			
Gold	4 - 3"	6 - 3"	10 - 3"
White	4 - 1½"	6 - 1½"	10 - 1½"
Gold	4 - 4"	6 - 5"	10 - 6"
Strips to Cut: Binding			
Gold	4 - 2½"	6 - 2½"	10 - 2½"

Ohio Star Construction

Refer to the section on *Using Easy Angle*™ and *Using Companion Angle*™ and cut the strips using the appropriate measurement on the tools. Sew white Easy Angle™ triangles onto the four sides of the square. Press the seam allowances toward the center.

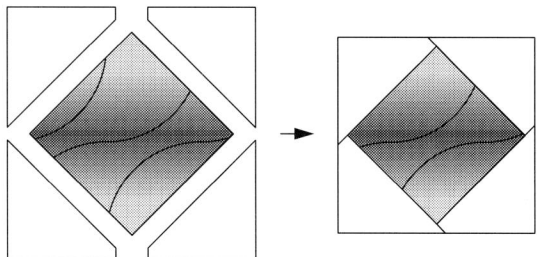

Sew the gold Easy Angle™ triangles to the sides of the Companion Angle™ triangles. Press these seam allowances toward the gold.

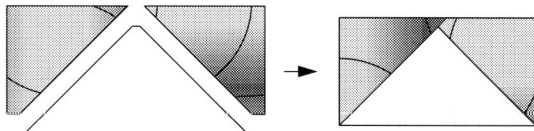

Join two of the above units to the center square. Press the seam allowance toward the points.

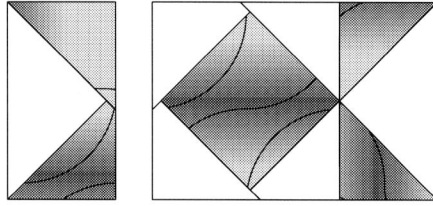

Sew a white square to either side of the other star points. Press the seams toward the star points.

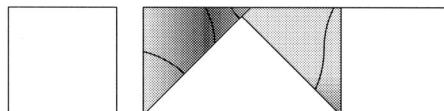

Sew these strips to the center block section. Press the seam toward the star points.

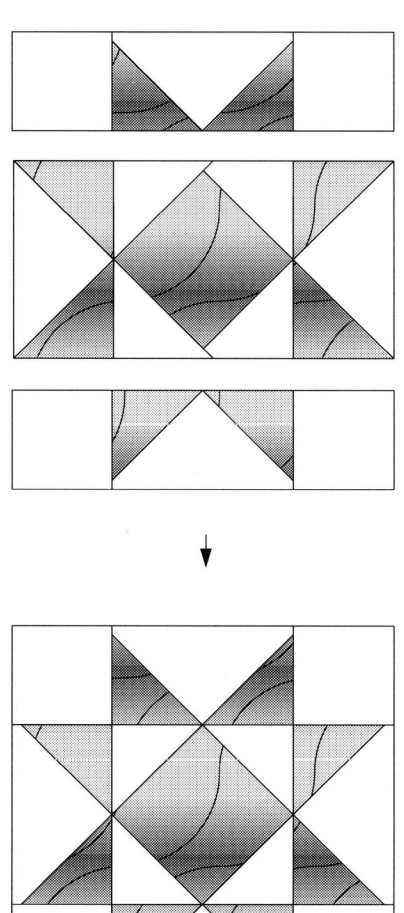

The graphic below shows the appropriate tool use for each star piece.

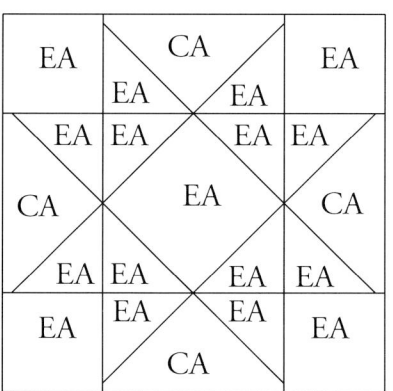

Happy-Go-Round
95" x 113"
See photo on page 33.

I found this wonderful scrap quilt in North Dakota. It is very thin but very heavy! By gently lifting open a seam where the stitches are broken I found the "batting" to be cotton grain sacks. The printing on the sacks is from an elevator in Bridgewater, SD. The quilt is tied with string. I'm sure the frost gathered on the top of this warm quilt many times. Note that the center hexagons are solid colors surrounded by pieces of fabric from clothing. The people in this family wore bright and happy colors! The quilt is hand pieced.

Tools Needed:
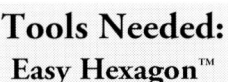

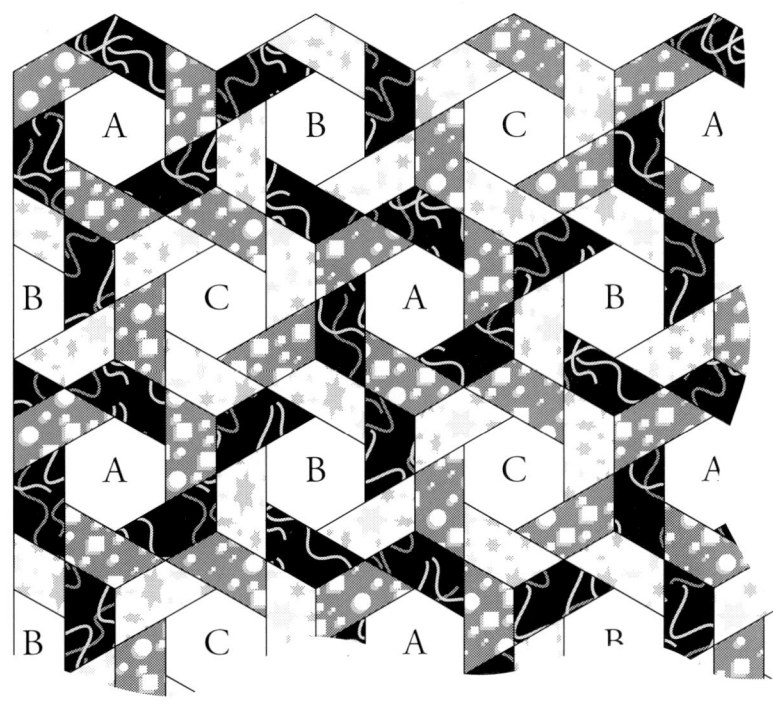

Happy-Go-Round Construction

The Happy-Go-Round blocks are made with a solid color hexagon center and then half hexagons surrounding it to form a larger hexagon. The finished edges of the center hexagon is 2". Follow the instructions in the *Using Easy Hexagon™* section of this book. The strips for the half-hexagons that surround the center are cut first on the 1" finished edge of the hexagon tool. If you are working with scrap pieces cut many strips before you begin sewing the larger hexagon unit.

Rotate the tool and slide the hexagon shape end of the tool to the left end of the fabric strip.

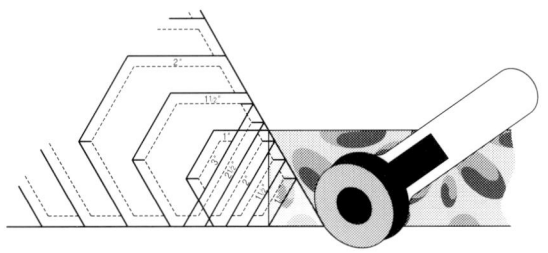

Cut the first angle, then flip the tool over and fill the 2" hexagon as shown below. Flip the tool back and continue to cut as many as possible from the strip.

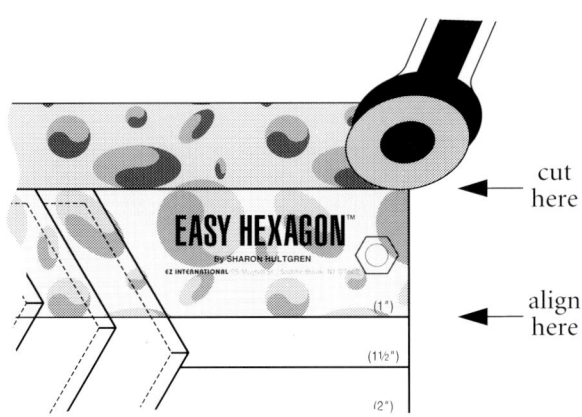

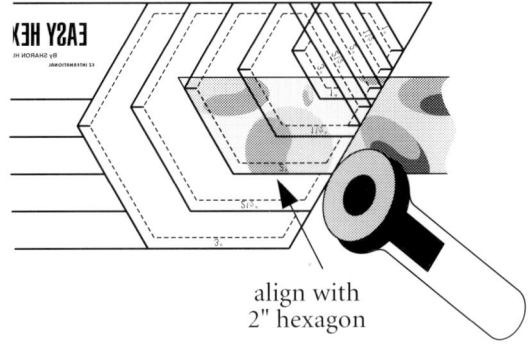

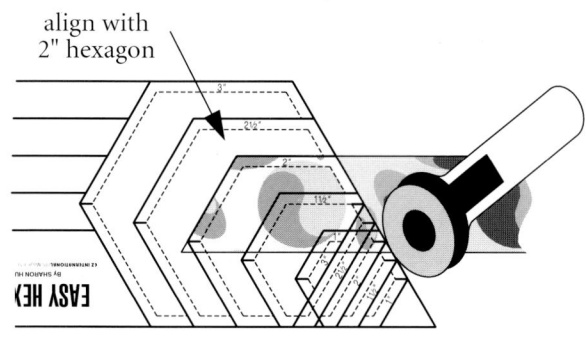

Begin sewing the first half-hex onto the solid hexagon. Begin in the middle of the half-hex. Stitch to the edge of the hexagon.

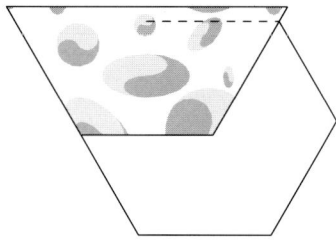

Turn the half-hex back and sew the next half-hex, etc. When all the half-hexes are sewn on, stitch the first piece again from one side to the other. This completed hexagon will measure 6¾" x 7¾".

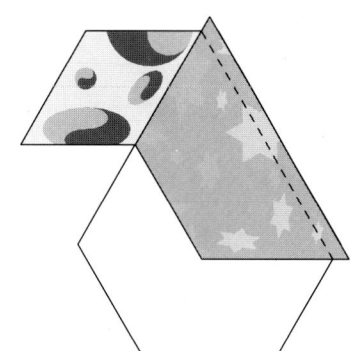

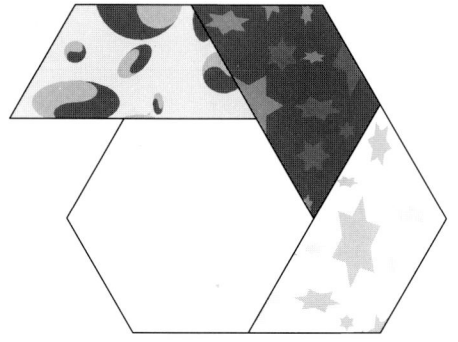

When you have completed the units set them out to establish the color pattern you like. To make a queen size quilt you will need 275 units – 10 rows of 14 hexagons and 9 rows of 15 hexagons.

If the center hexagon were made of muslin, this would make an outstanding signature quilt! A perfect wedding gift, with the signature of all the quests at the wedding.

Happy-Go-Round can also be an exciting planned quilt. By using three different colors around a light solid hexagon you can create a woven pattern.

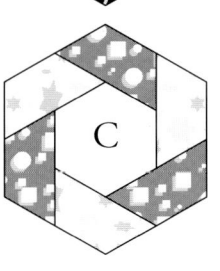

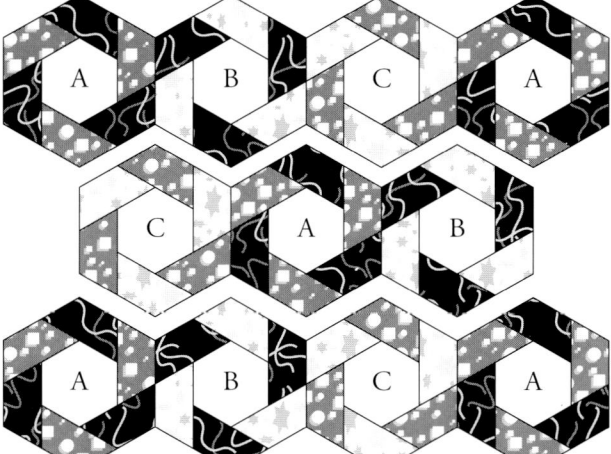

Begin sewing the hexagon rows together. Leave the seam open at the top and the bottom. Join the next row in the same way. Then join the two rows together. Continue until you have all the blocks sewn into rows.

Fabric Requirements 95" x 113":	
Background	4 yards
Color one	4 yards
Color two	4 yards
Color three	4 yards

Jacob's Ladder Variation
89" x 103"

Winter Pines Table Cover
60" across

Cabin in the Woods
59" x 74"
Does this look like someplace you would like to be?

Garden Flower Update (circa 1930)
60" x 72"

The edges of this antique quilt were appliquéd onto the border. The quilting is done in a zig-zag line from side to side rather than around each petal.

Stars All Around (circa 1920)
64" x 80"

This antique quilt is a good example of using scraps with a solid background. This quilt has been well used!

Wedding Ring (circa 1930)
88" x 106"
Quilt top found in near perfect condition, now quilted and ready to use! Inset to the right shows more detail.

Happy-Go-Round (circa 1930)
78" x 96"
This antique quilt is easier than it looks! Inset to the left shows more detail.

One Sunday Morning

You can almost see the sun coming through the glass!

Inner City, The Easy Way!

"Take Your Stand, Yes, M'am"

Ohio Star (circa 1920)
50" x 78"
This antique summer quilt shows how really great a two color quilt can be!

Spinning Spools
Each block is 18" with the sashing.

Windy Hill
Tied and ready to snuggle under!

From My Attic Window
46" x 54"

Attic Window Memory
46" x 46"

Nora's Star
68" x 76"
Made by my grandmother, Nora Laird May, in 1950.

One Sunday Morning

See photo on page 34.

This entire quilt is made using the Easy Eight™ and a straight edge ruler such as Quickline™.

The center star is made by cutting on the 2" finished line.

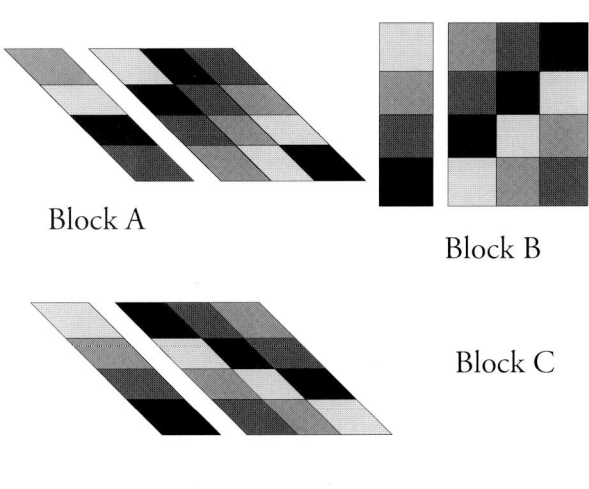

Block A

Block B

Block C

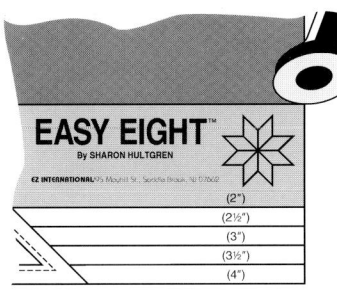

Sew the strips together in the same way as *Nora's Star*. However, there will be four strips in each of four combinations. These are then sewn together to make the large star.

The squares are made of 2½" squares sewn together into an 8" finished block. The corner diamonds are made from diamonds cut with the Easy Eight™ on the 2" finished mark.

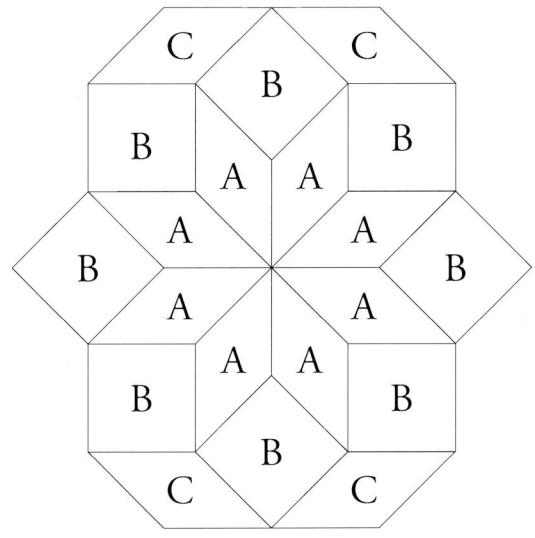

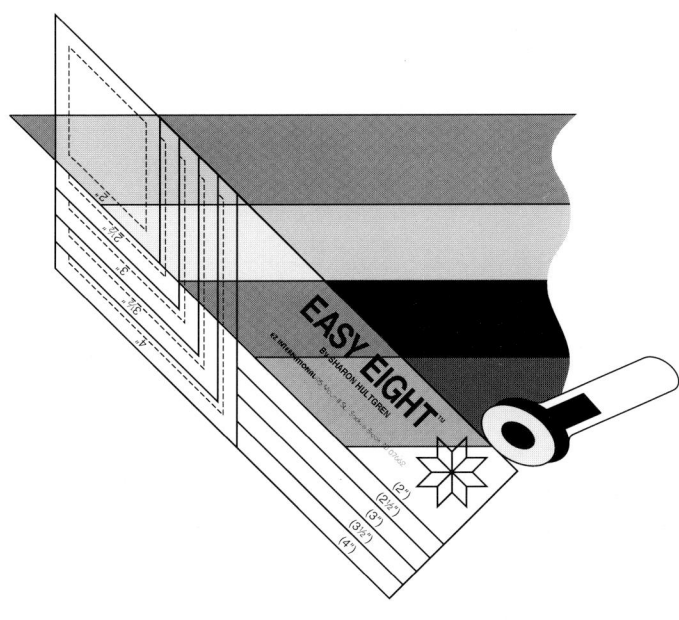

Wedding Ring

94½" x 102½" without border
See photo on page 32.

Tools Needed:
Easy Six™
Easy Hexagon™

Making this quilt is like eating popcorn! One star leads to the next! Don't let the numbers scare you! The design is a combination of six-pointed stars and hexagons. The sides of two stars equals one side of the hexagon. The quilt shown uses a 1½" finished edge on the Easy Six™ and the 3" finished edge of the Easy Hexagon™. This quilt is made from your treasure chest of scraps. Have fun sharing scraps with your friends!

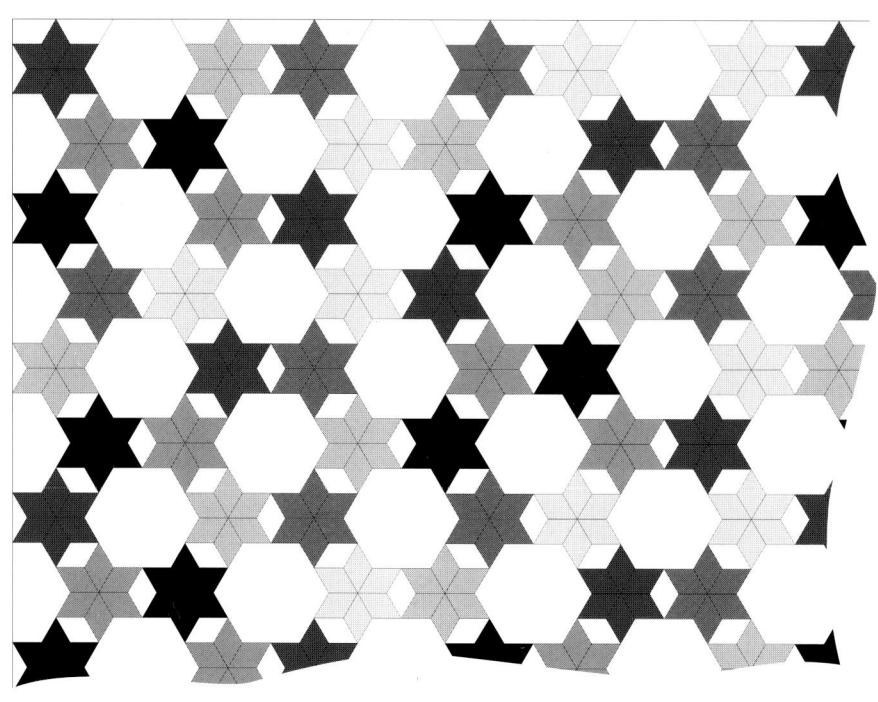

Fabric Requirements:

378 six pointed stars	6 yards
567 connecting diamonds	1¾ yards
199 center hexagons	7 yards

For each *Wedding Ring* unit make six stars (step 1). (Note six pointed star directions.) Join the stars with a background diamond (step 2). The quilt on page 32 shows the stars are joined by colorful diamonds. Set a hexagon into the center of the ring (step 3). Join rings in a row, connecting them with a background diamond (step 4). Join rows with background diamond stars. Set in connecting background hexagons (step 6). This could be a grand signature quilt! Let friends and family have their own circle of stars!

There are five rows of seven complete rings across. There are four rows of six complete rings with a half ring on either end.

Note: If you use two fabrics in each star you will need a piece that is only 1⅞" x 8" for each color. Start saving scraps from anywhere and everywhere!

Piecing the Six Pointed Star

Cut six 1½" finished diamonds using the Easy Six™.

Sew four of these into two pairs. When sewing these leave the seam open above the seam intersection. An accurate ¼" seam is a must!

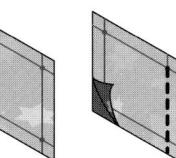

Press the pairs on the right side of the fabric. The seams must go toward the left.

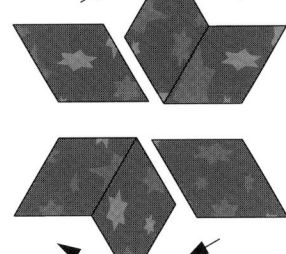

Add a third diamond to each pair. Again press the seam toward the left while pressing on the right side of the fabric. Sew the top half to the bottom half. Leave both the beginning and the end of the seam open.

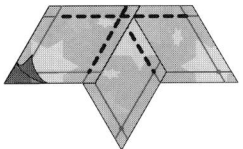

To set the side diamonds into the star begin sewing on the left side sewing toward the center, matching seam intersections. Then sew the right side, stitching toward the center. Press seams toward the star.

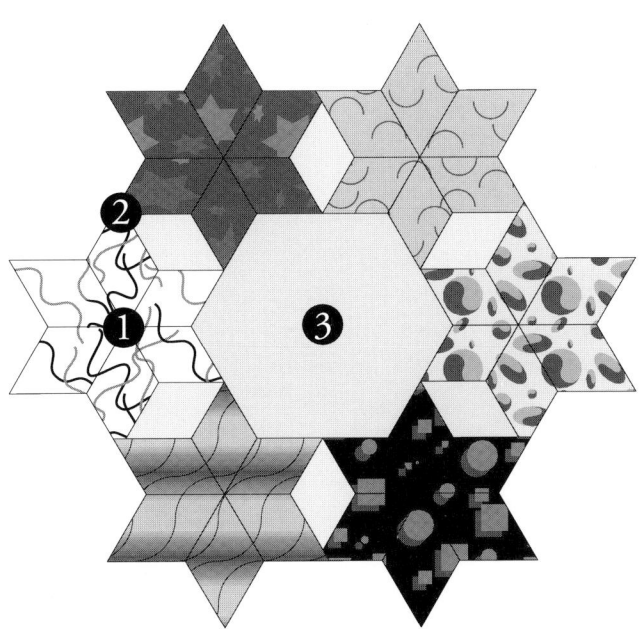

After piecing the stars and setting in the diamonds to make the ring of six stars, the next step is to set in the hexagon in the center of the ring. After the hexagon is set in, sew the blocks in rows as shown below.

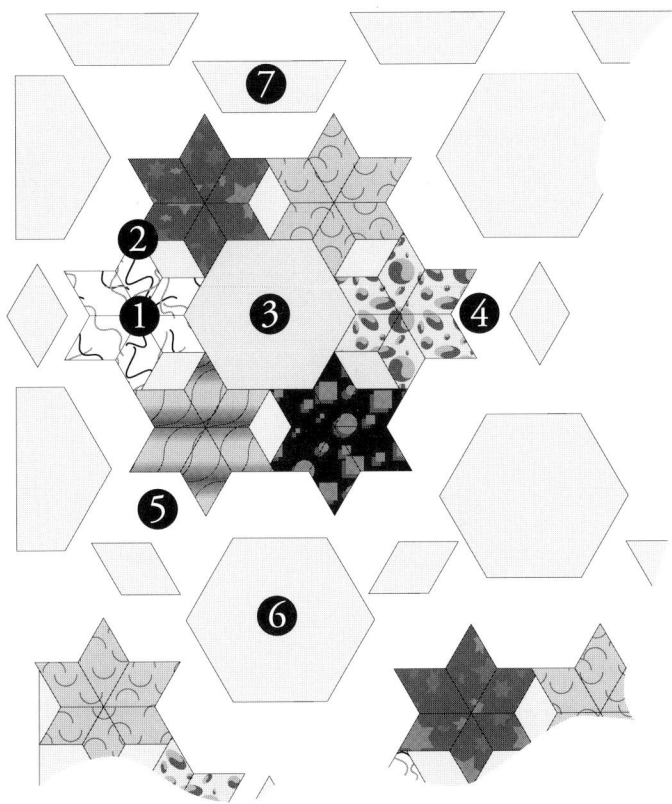

Numbers represent construction steps from the preceding page.

Finishing

To finish the outside edge of the quilt, cut strips on the 1½" finished edge of the Easy Six™. Use the Easy Hexagon™ to cut these into correct lengths as needed. (Step 7 above.)

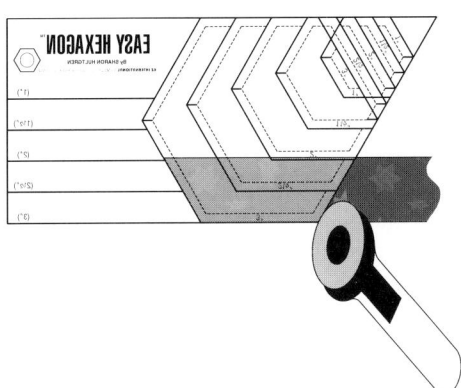

Inner City, The Easy Way!

See photo on page 35.

Tools Needed:
Easy Hexagon™

Fabric Requirements:

½ yard of three fabrics
1 yard of black background

This quilt is easy to make when using the Easy Hexagon™. The drama of the quilt is made by the placement of three shades of fabric. The fabrics can be the same as seen in the picture or they could be three values of many colors.

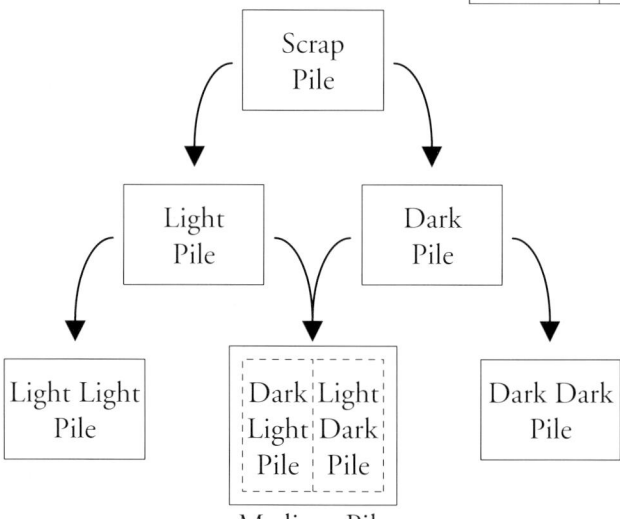

The easy way to sort your scrap fabric into three values of color is to first make two piles of your scraps, light and dark. Now sort the light pile into a light and dark pile. Then sort the dark pile into a dark and light pile. The dark fabrics from the light pile and the light fabrics from the dark pile become your medium pile. Follow the chart to the left to help sort your scraps.

42

If you use three set colors for the quilt hanging, you will need six strips of each color cut on the Easy Hexagon™ 1½" line. You will get six hexagon pieces from each strip.

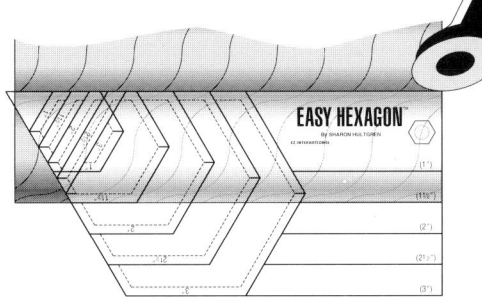

Now follow the 3" finished edge on the Easy Hexagon™ and cut hexagons from these strips.

After you cut the hexagons arrange them on a flannel wall, bed or the floor. Then begin to sew them side by side (as shown in the larger graphic at bottom of page). When the rows are complete join them together. Remember when sewing hexagons together you must leave the seam open ¼" on the top and bottom.

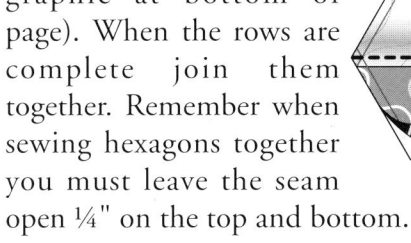

To add a little interest, it is fun to set a hexagon of the background fabric here and there.

To finish the edges on the wallhanging, I sewed a black piece to the pieced top, leaving a small opening, and then turned it.

Sew the strips into the following combinations.

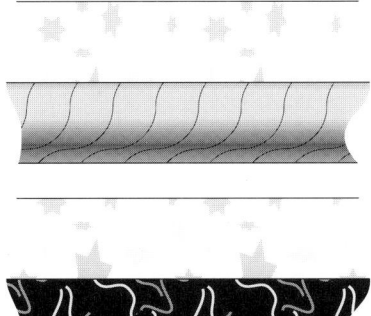

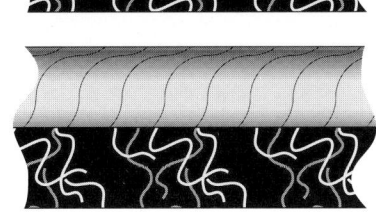

Sew hexagons together in rows.

43

Take Your Stand, Yes Ma'm!

See photo on page 35.

This wall quilt is made in the shape of *Seven Sisters*. It is made in celebration of the early detection of my mother's breast cancer. The fabric in the center of each star (see photo) is printed as a fund raiser for the mammagram program sponsered by *Quilt America*.

Tools Needed:
Easy Hexagon™

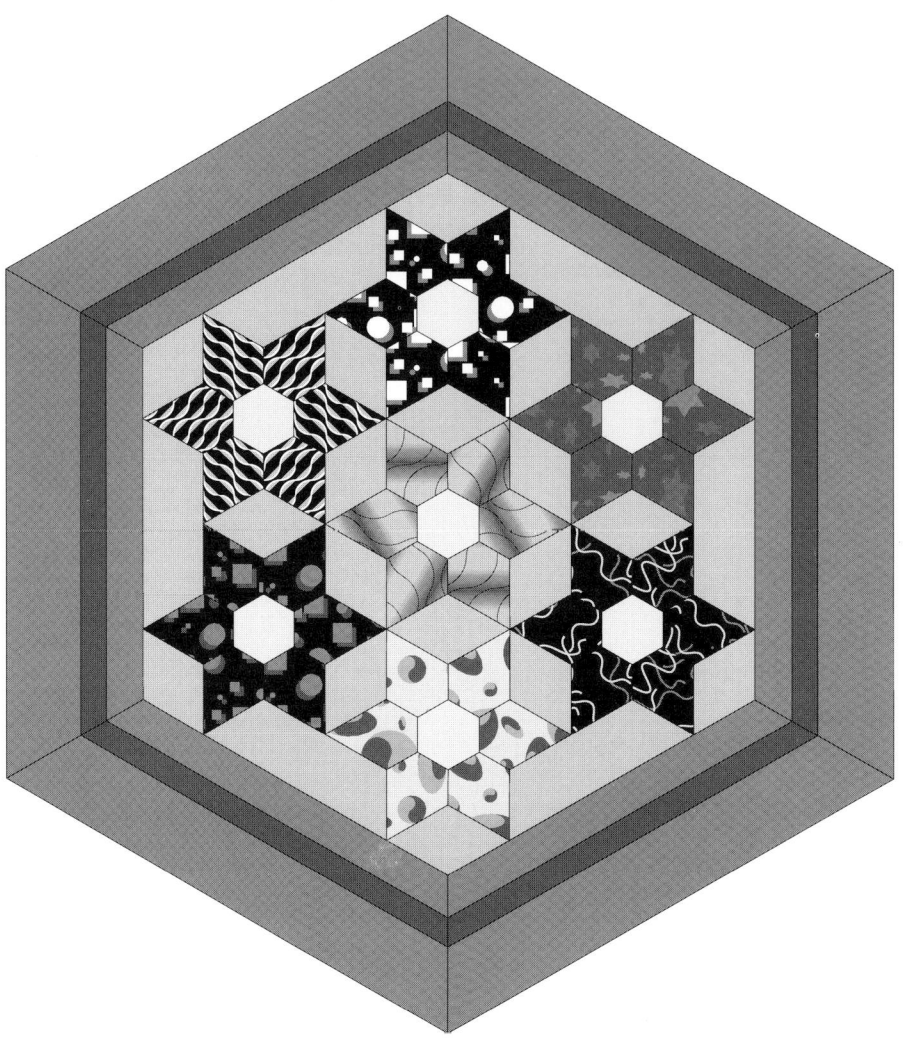

Fabric Requirements:

Red	1 yd OR
	7 - ⅛ yds
Border accent	¼ yd
Border & Binding	1 yd
Background	¾ yd

Using the Easy Hexagon™, cut a strip from the star center fabric following the 1½" marking. Cut seven hexagons.

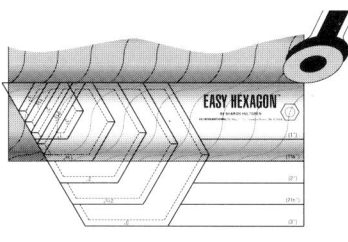

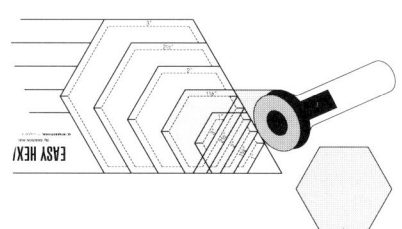

Cut a strip on the same mark (1½") from seven different reds or fabric you have chosen. Cut six diamond shapes from each strip. Cut only one of the points off, leaving an ice cream cone shape. Also cut 8 background diamonds on the 1½" line.

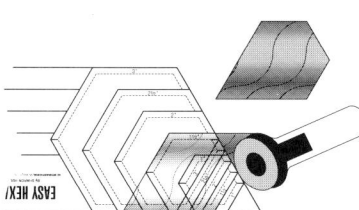

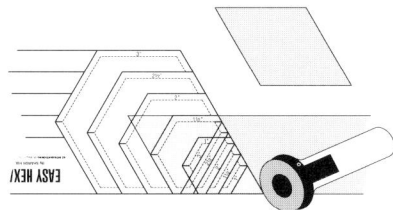

44

Arrange the flower as shown and sew pieces together in the order given. Leave the seam open at the top and bottom of each seam in the Star. Make seven stars.

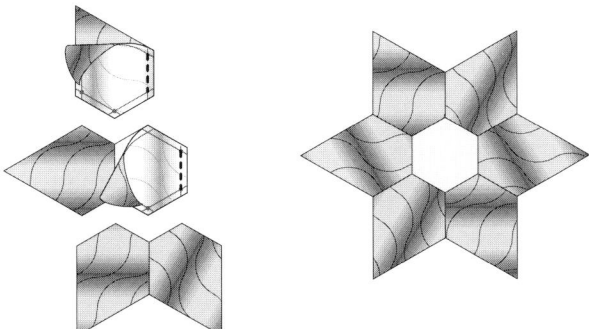

Set six of the diamonds around the center star.

Make six more stars. These are connected by a background diamond to form a ring.

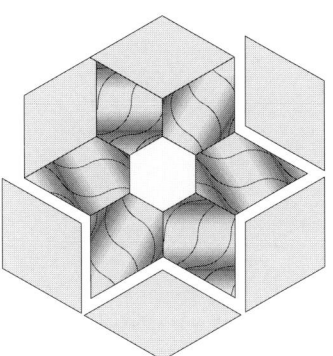

Join the stars by sewing a diamond to one star and then to it's neighbor. Continue around the ring. When the ring is complete, set in the center star. Set background diamonds into the stars on the outside of the ring.

Cut two strips of background fabric on the 1½" marking. Make one angle cut.

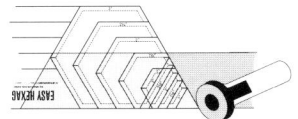

On the seam line, measure 6". Cut the other angle as shown. Be sure to include the seam allowance after the 6" mark. Cut six pieces like this. Try one, and make sure it fits before cutting all six. Set these into the star ring as shown.

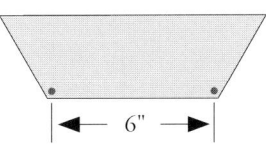

Borders

Cut 3 -2" strips of blue; cut three 1½" strips of red; cut three 3½" strips of blue. Sew these together in three sets in the exact order given for cutting.

Cut each set in half. Find the center of the border and the center of each side of the quilt. Measure the sides for the quilt and use one of the measurements for each border piece. All of the edges must be even for the quilt to hang nicely. Miter the corners with the Easy Hexagon™.

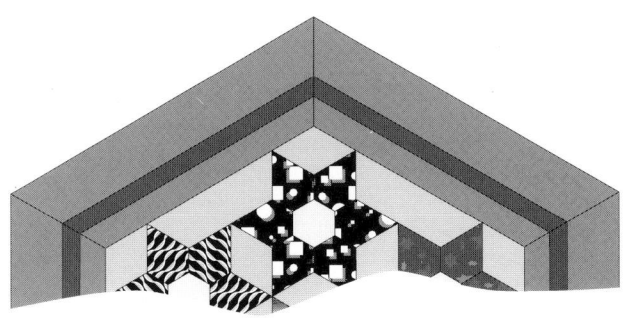

Easy Grandmother's Flower Garden

88" x 110"
See photo on page 30.

Whenever the name *Grandmother's Flower Garden* crosses someone's lips, most quilters utter a quiet "wow!" The smallest pieces of fabric basted over pieces of newsprint and then hand sewn side-by-side is how these beauteous wonders were begun in times past. I tried one once and ended up with a very small bun basket. After a trip to England I was determined to try again! With the knowledge of how the Easy Six™ worked, I was sure we could make hexagons in the same way. Yes! It worked! Hexagons are as easy as diamonds and even prettier. (Note instructions for the use of the Easy Hexagon™.) When piecing the hexagons it is important to be very aware of the seam intersections. These must meet, and for the most part we stitch only up to them, not over them! Leave 1½" threads on each end of the seam. If you want to backstitch be very careful that you do not stitch into the seam allowance. The hexagons given in this pattern are cut on the 2" finished edge of the Easy Hexagon™.

Consider making flower units, one row at a time. Then place these flower units next to another one until you have as many joined as you like. The next row will be joined the same way and then the rows will be joined with many short seams. It does seem like a lot of work but the finished product is worth it!

Note the way the quilt in the picture is finished. We all groan when we think about putting on the binding. The lady who made this quilt solved the problem by sewing the outside hexagons directly onto the border, thus having a straight edge. Like many old quilts, a second border is not used.

Tools Needed:
Easy Hexagon™

Fabric Requirements: 28 full flowers and 4 half flowers		Fabric Requirements: each Flower unit	
Cream background	5 yds	Dark print	⅛ yd (6 Hexagons)
Yellow centers	¾ yd	Light print	¼ yd (12 Hexagons)
Light print OR Thirty-two Prints	5½ yds OR ¼ yd each	1 Hexagon for center flower	
Dark print OR Thirty-two Prints	3½ yds OR ⅛ yd each	1 strip for light background (8 Hexagons)	

Flower Garden Construction

Cut strips on the 2" finished edge of the Easy Hexagon™ tool.

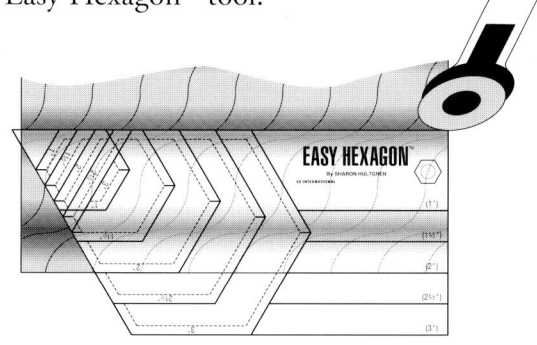

Cut hexagons as shown in the *Tool Tutorial*.

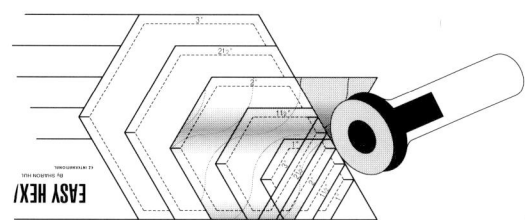

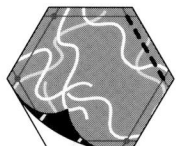 Place hexagons right sides together and sew between the seam intersections. *Do not sew past the seam allowances when putting these hexagons together.*

Sew hexagons together in rows as indicated. There will be six rows for each block. When cut on a 2" finished edge, the flower units will be 18" x 21".

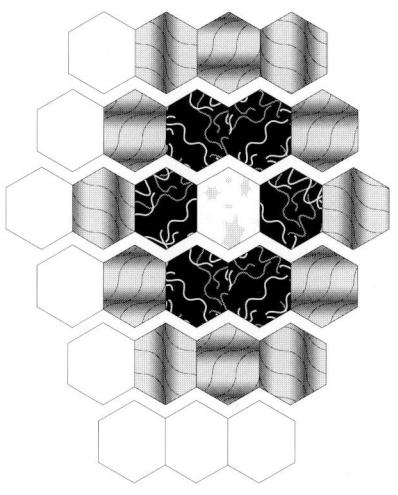

Place the blocks together in rows and sew the rows together as indicated below.

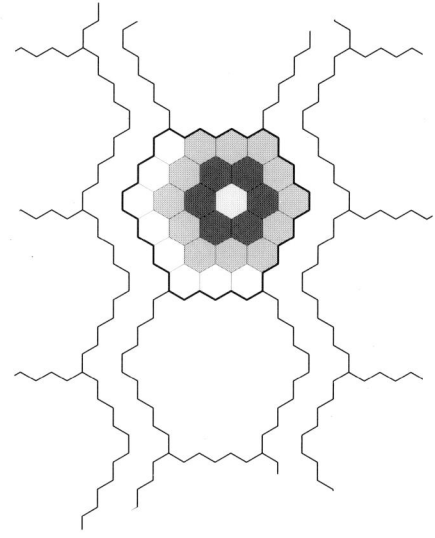

47

Stars All Around
See photo on page 31.

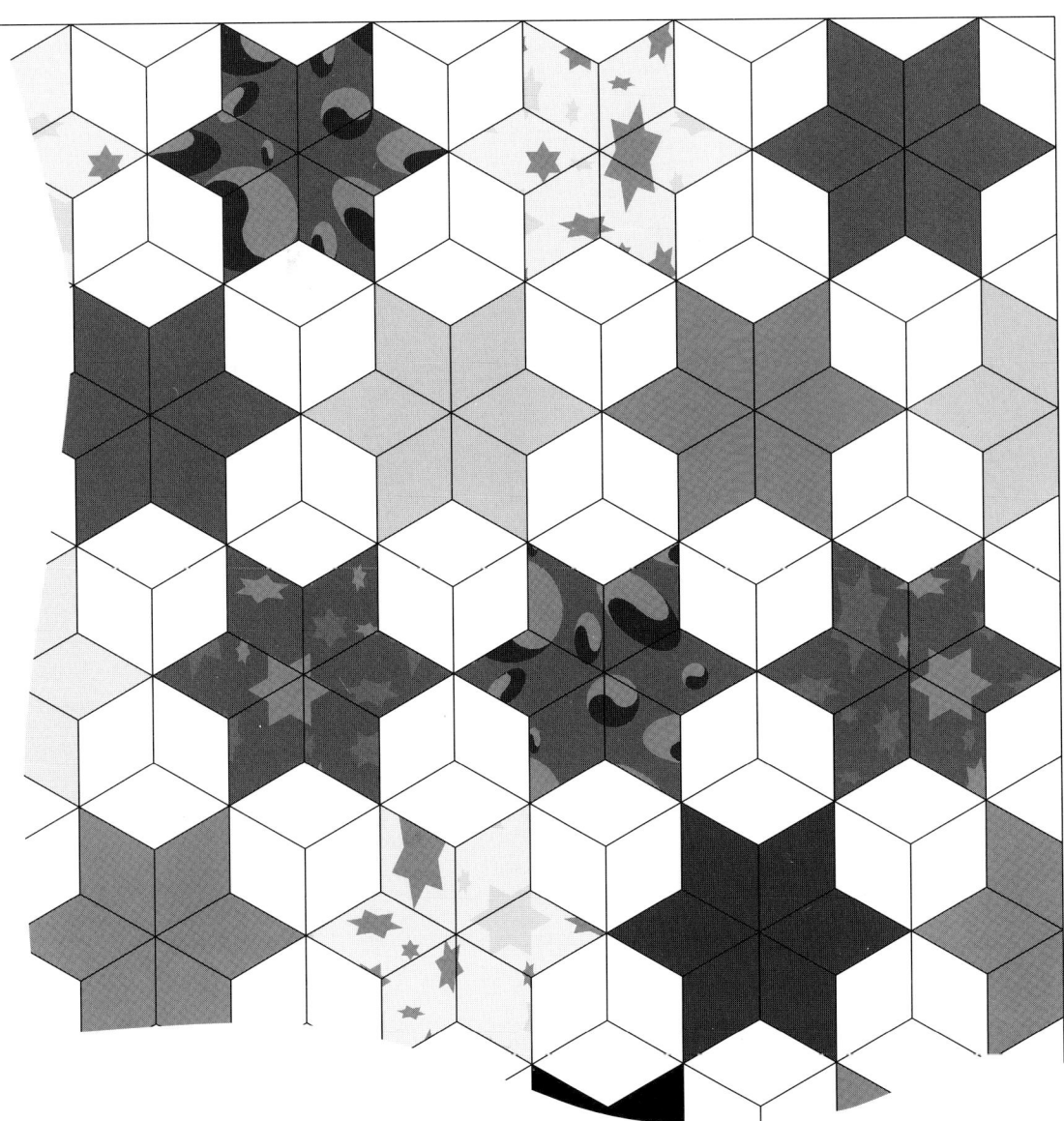

This is another fun scrap quilt. First piece the six pointed stars. Then surround the star with diamonds from the background fabric. This will create a large hexagon. When the star hexagons come together the background diamonds will form a hexagon. This will cause the stars to float on the background. This would make an outstanding two color quilt.

Fabric Requirements: 66" x 72" Fireside 46 full stars; 6 half stars	
Stars	3 yds
Background	3 yds
Binding	¾ yds

Tools Needed: Easy Six™

Fabric Requirements: 84" x 102" Queen 86 full stars; 8 half stars	
Stars	5½ yds
Background	5½ yds
Binding	1 yd

Stars All Around Construction

Cut strips for the stars on the 2" finished edge line of the Easy Six™ tool. The number of strips depends on the number of different stars you will make. Cut background strips to equal the total number of the star fabric strips,

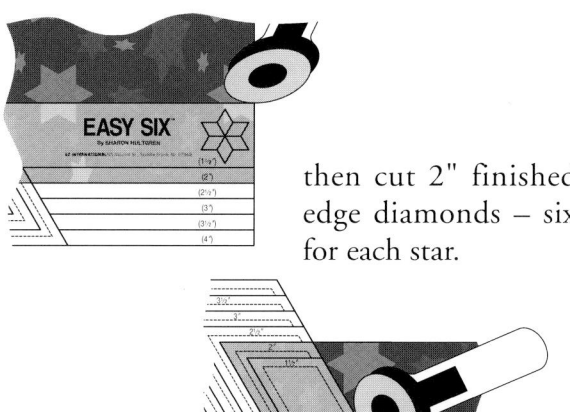

then cut 2" finished edge diamonds – six for each star.

Make stars using the method shown in the *Wedding Ring* project. Add background diamonds around each star as shown below.

Finished block shown below.

Sew stars together in rows. Place stars right sides together and sew along one edge. Sew only between points where seam allowances intersect. For the 66" x 72" quilt, sew four rows of seven stars and three rows of six. At each end of the rows of six, add a half star (bottom half at the top and top half at the bottom.)

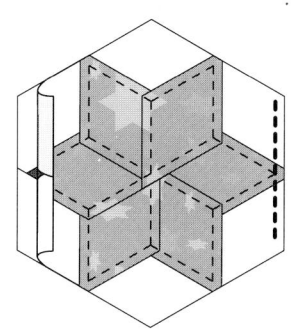

Combine the rows, starting with a row of seven and alternating with the rows of 6, ending with a row of 7. Trim background diamonds or add as necessary to even the edges of the quilt (see the graphic on the preceding page.) For the 84" x 102" quilt make 5 rows of 10 stars and 4 rows of 9 stars. Attach half-stars at the top and bottom of the shorter rows.

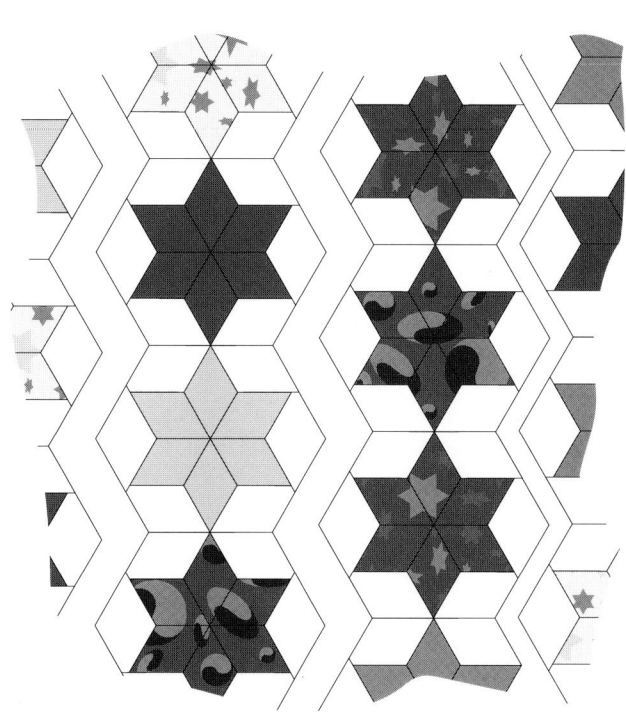

Windy Hill
62" x 74"
See photo on page 36.

This is a super fast, super easy quilt. Yardage is given for a baby, fireside and queen size quilt. The windmill is made of four blocks that are turned clockwise.

Tools Needed:
Easy Angle II™
Companion Angle II™

Windy Hill Construction

Cut a 6½" strip of fabric "A". Use the Easy Angle II™ to cut triangles. These can be cut with the fabric folded in half. You will get twelve per strip.

Cut a 3½" strip of both B and C. Place these fabrics right sides together (they will be ready to sew together) and cut with the Companion Angle™. You will get nine per strip.

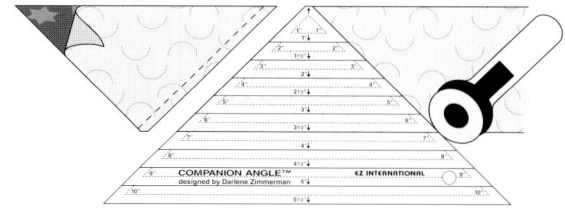

Sew a short side of one triangle to a short side of the other fabric. Sew these to the A triangle. Make 4 of these blocks and rotate them clockwise to create the *Windy Hill* block.

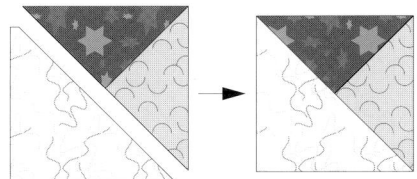

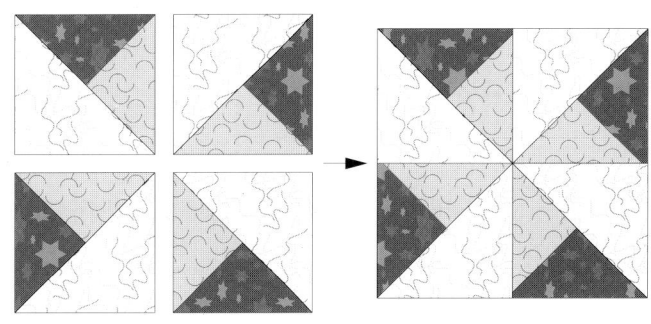

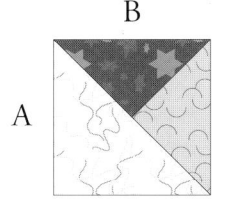

The yardage chart below gives the requirements for three sizes of quilts. No mater which size you make you will need three fabrics, labeled A, B, C, The graphic to the left shows the relative placement of each fabric.

Fabric Requirements:				
Fabric	**Strip Width**	**A**	**B**	**C**
Crib	38" x 50"	1½ yds	¾ yd	1 yd
Fireside	62" x 72"	3¼ yds	1¼ yds	1¾ yds
Queen	98 x 110"	5¾ yds	3 yds	3½ yds
Number of Blocks and Strips to Cut:				
Fabric	**Strip width**	**A (6½")**	**B (3½")**	**C (3½")**
Crib	2 x 3	2	3	3
Fireside	4 x 5	7	9	9
Queen	7 x 8	9	25	25
Border Strips to Cut:				
		A (4½")	**B (1½")**	**C (2½")**
Crib		5 yds	5 yds	5 yds
Fireside		8 yds	8 yds	8 yds
Queen		10 yds	10 yds	10 yds

From My Attic Window
46" x 54"
See photo on page 37.

Do you see stars when you look out your attic window? You can when this quilt is hanging on you wall! First make the simple Friendship Star and then frame it with perfect attic windows. By cutting the strips different widths, the windows can be as small as 4" or as large as 8". The technique used to frame the stars can also be used to frame other squares such as solid fabric for quilting or pictures of your friends and family. I have found that it is good to use a thin accent border around the windows like a window frame. The top and side of windows need a place to stop.

Tools Needed:
Easy Angle™
Easy Angle II™

Friendship Star Construction

Cut a 2½" strip of cream. Cut a 2½" strip of blue. Place these fabrics right sides together. and cut 4 triangles with the Easy Angle™. Sew the triangles together.

Cut five 2½" squares of cream. Set the squares together with the triangle blocks previously

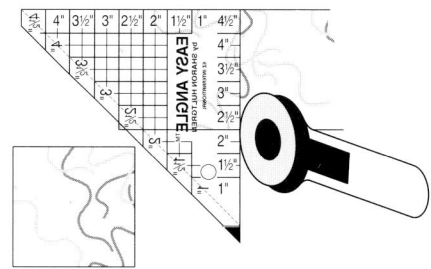

Sew the squares together and then sew together into rows.

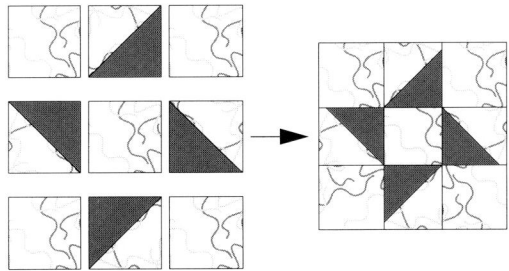

Window Frame Construction

The window frame is made using the Easy Angle II™. Cut a 2½" strip from each of the window frame fabrics. It is important that the fabric you place on top continues in that position as you cut more window frames. Our attic window block will be 8" finished.

Place the Easy Angle II™ so that the 8½" marking is completely on the fabric. Cut the diagonal edge.

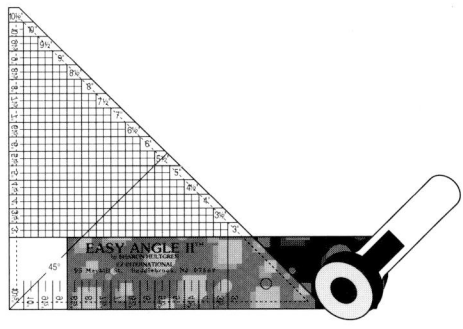

Flip the tool over and place the Easy Angle II™ so that the 8½" is on the fabric again.

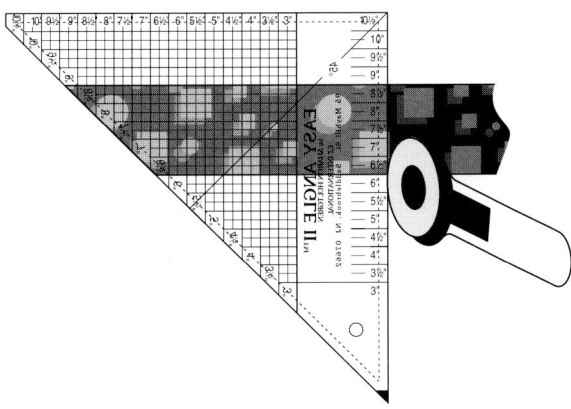

Sew the window frames together. Leave the seam open on the shorter side.

Set the Friendship Star into the window frame. Sew from the top down, stop when you come to the diagonal seam; backstitch. Start again on the right side and stitch the bottom frame toward the diagonal seam. The outside edges should be even.

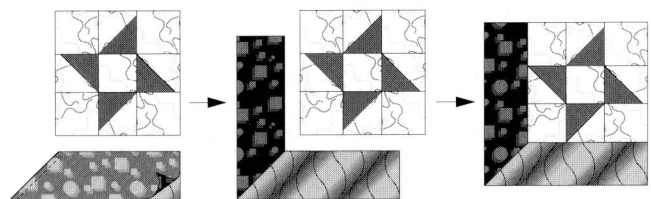

Use this framing technique for any size window frame. The strip can be cut any width. The total block size will be the size of the square plus the width of the window frame.

(1" fin.   (3" fin.
1½" unfin.) 3½" unfin.)

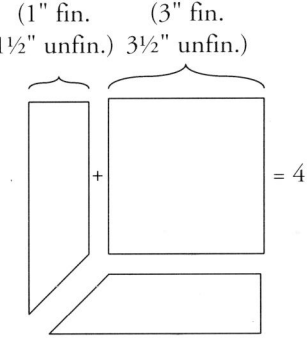

Join blocks together. Cut accent fabric into 1½" strips. Add these around the blocks. Cut five 6½" strips for the outside border. Join together as needed.

Fabric Requirements:	
Stars	½ yd
Sky & Binding	¾ yd
Window Side	¾ yd
Window Bottom	¾ yd
Accent Frame	⅜ yd
Outside Border	1 yd

Spinning Spools

See photo on page 36.

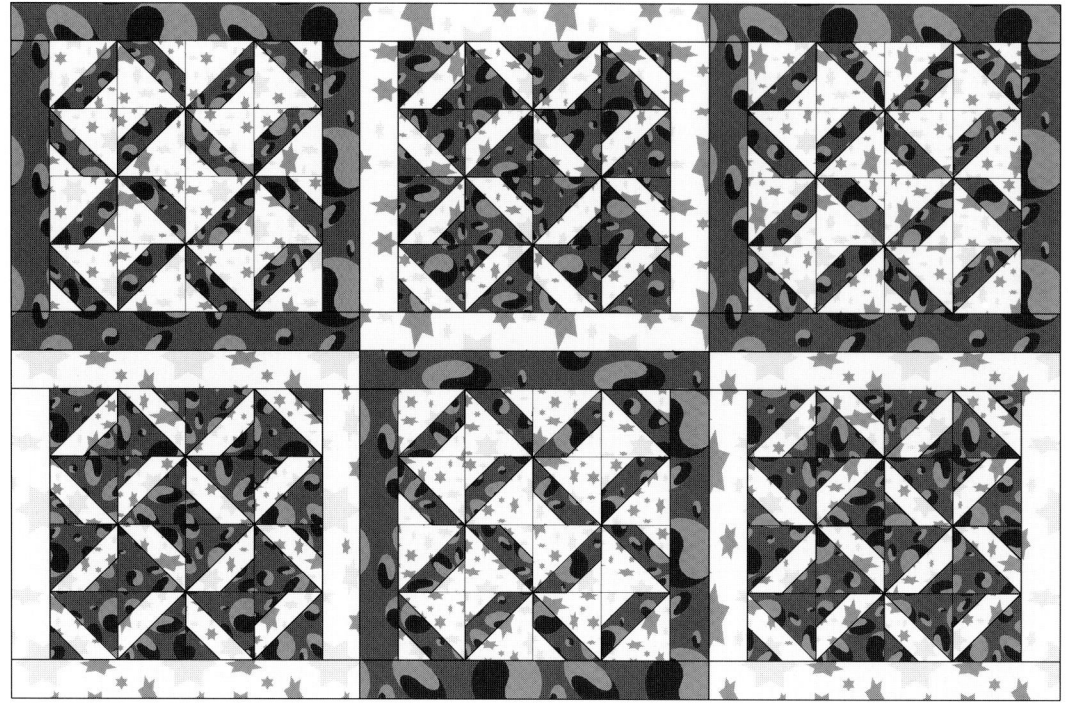

Spool Construction

Cut one 4" strip of both the dark and light. Cut one 1¾" strip of both the dark and light. Sew the two narrow strips together. Press the seam toward the dark strip.

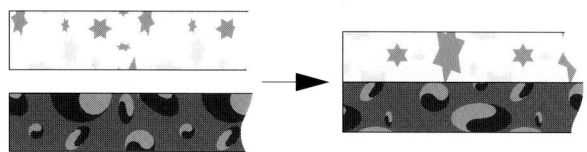

Using the Companion Angle™ cut triangles from the sewn strip.

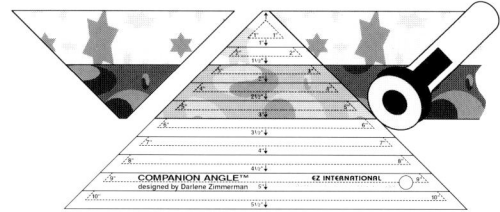

Using Easy Angle™, cut right angle triangles from the 4" strips.

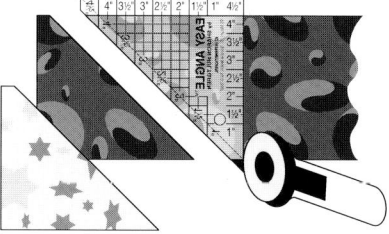

Sew the triangles together! You will watch the Spools spin right before your eyes!! Note how the colorations fit together.

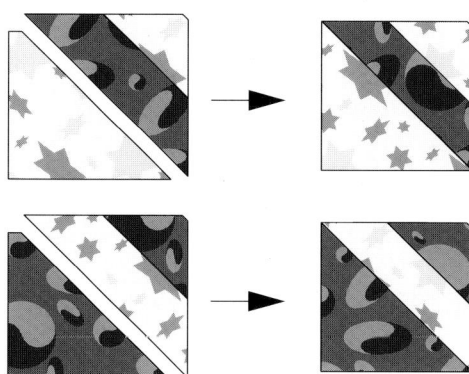

54

There are four spool squares in each large block. The border around each square is cut 2½". Each block is bordered as shown.

Ruffle Construction

Putting a ruffle on your quilt is optional. This is done after the quilt is quilted. To make a ruffle for the lap quilt, cut 10 -9" strips. Sew these together end to end. Sew long sides together to make a long tube. Turn and press. One inch from one side zigzag over a gathering string. Gather this and stitch to the top of the quilt. Prepare the quilt by finishing the raw edges with satin stitching.

Tools Needed:
Easy Angle™
Companion Angle™

Fabric Requirements:		
Lap	**Fireside**	**Queen**
2 x 3 Blocks	3 x 4 Blocks	5 x 6 Blocks
36" x 54"	54" x 72"	90" x 108"
1½ yds dark	3 yds dark	7 yds dark
1½ yds light	3 yd light	7 yds light
2¾ yds Ruffle (optional)	¾ yd Binding	1 yd Binding
Strips to Cut:		
3 - 4" light	6 - 4" light	15 - 4" light
3 - 4" dark	6 - 4" dark	15 - 4" dark
12 - 1¾" light	24 - 1¾" light	48 - 1¾" light
12 - 1¾" dark	24 - 1¾" dark	48 - 1¾" dark
6 - 2½" light border	12 - 2½" light border	30 - 2½" light border
6 - 2½" dark border	12 - 2½" dark border	30 - 2½" dark border

Jacob's Ladder
89" x 103"
See photo on page 37.

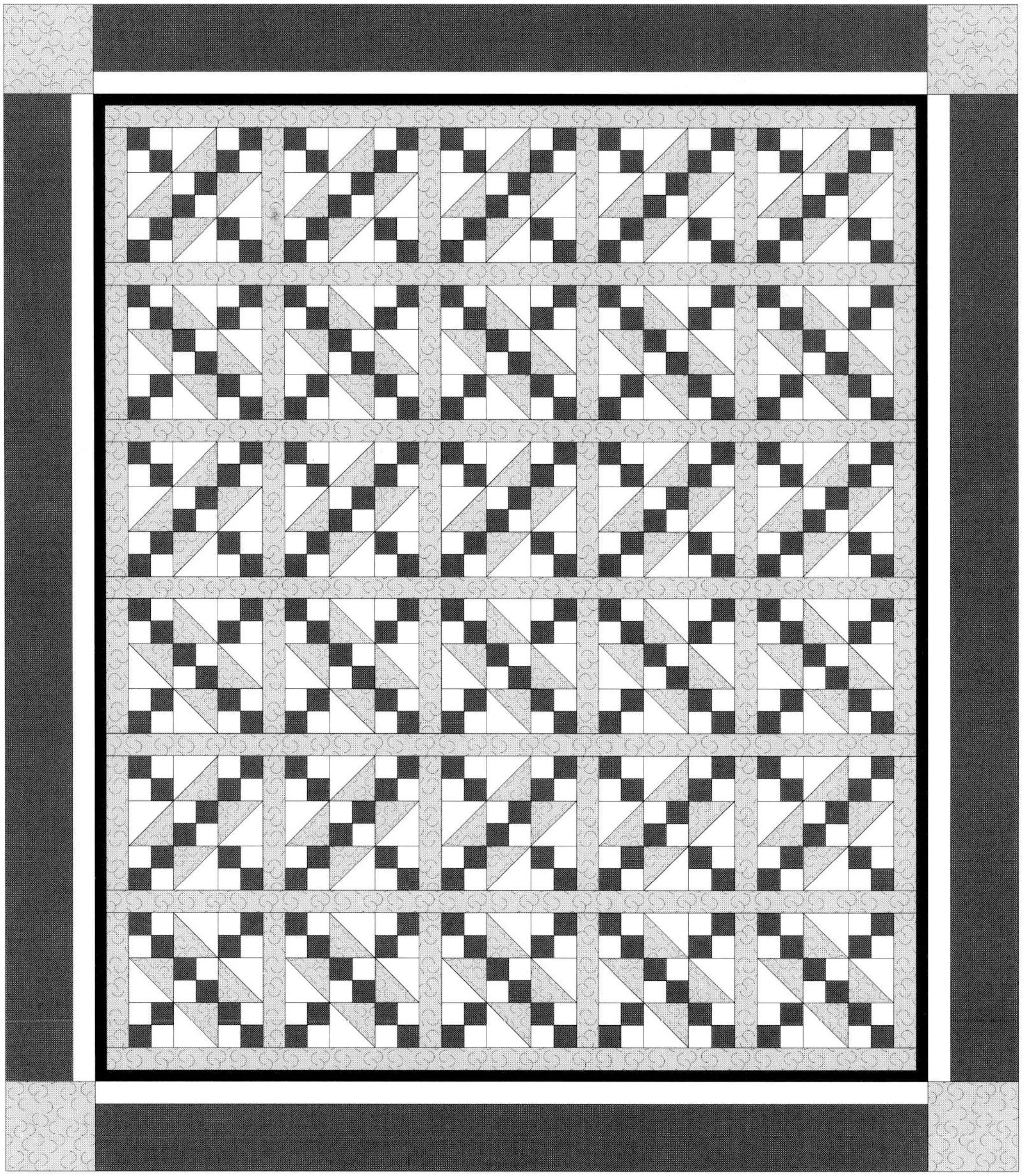

Ladder Construction

Stitch the white and light blue strips together, press seams toward the blue, then counter-cut into 300 -2½" units.

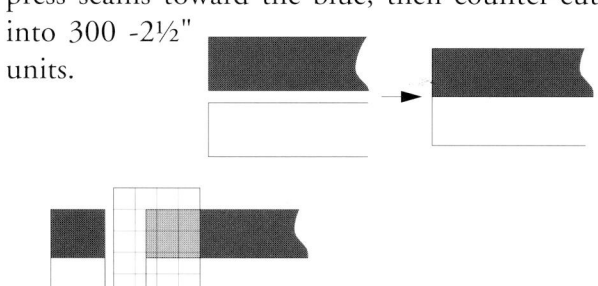

Sew these together into pairs to make 150 four-patch squares.

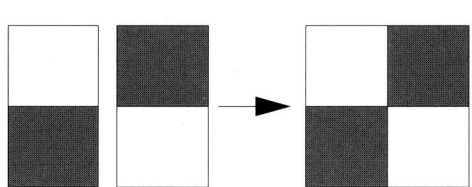

Place eight white and light blue strips together, then using the Easy Angle™ cut into 120 triangle units. Sew these together along the diagonal, then press seams toward the blue.

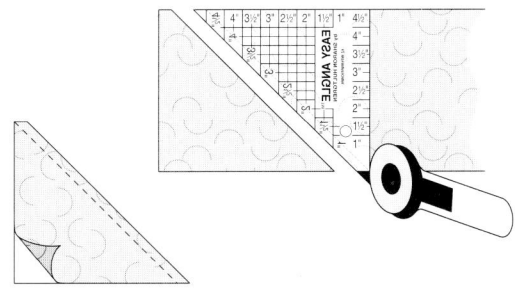

Sew these units into the Jacob's Ladder block as shown. Note that there are two settings for the blocks. The block is pieced the same way, but it "rolled over" to create the zigzag effect.

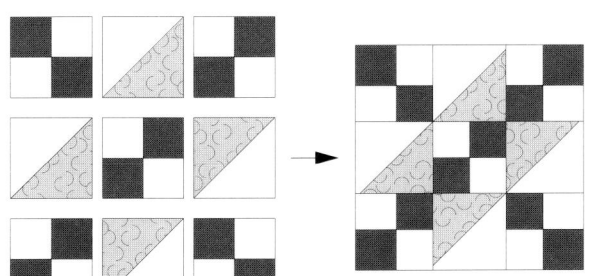

"Rolled over" block.

Tools Needed:
Easy Angle™

Sashing

Take your light blue sashing strips and that have been counter-cut into 12½" x 2½" strips and sew between blocks and at the end of each row of blocks.

Sew seven pairs of 2½" strips end to end and place one of these longer strips between rows of blocks, and at the top and bottom of the quilt before any borders are added. These strips should be trimmed to 72½".

When you combine rows, remember to alternate the orientation of the blocks in a zigzag fashion.

Fabric Requirements:		
Fabric	**Strips**	**Width to Cut**
White	8	4½"
Blue	8	4½"
White	19	4½"
Dark blue	19	2½"
Light blue Sashing	2	12½"*
Light blue Sashing	15	2½"**
Accent	8	1½"
White Borders	8	2½"
Dk blue Borders	8	6½"
Lt blue Borders	1	8½"
(*counter-cut into 12½" x 2½" strips)		
(**counter-cut one of these into 12½" strips)		

Nora's Star
77" x 97"
See photo on page 38.

This quilt was made by my grandmother, Nora Laird May. Her family lived in Metropolis, IL. She would have enjoyed the wonderful AQS quilt show in Paducah, KY., right across the river from her home. She was the only quilter in my family, and passed away before my interest in quilting was born. The colors seen here are really very bright. I'm sure working on this made her happy. Note that the quilt in the photo on page 38 is square. I have extended it so it will fit our beds better. To do this you should make four rows of the large stars, five rows of the small stars, and add 1", 4" and 6" borders.

Tools Needed:
Easy Angle™
Easy Angle II™ • Easy Eight™

Fabric Requirements 77" x 97":

Background (cream)	2 yards
Pink border & Sashing	4 yards
Yellow (or your choice)	1 yard
Floral print & Accent	2½ yards
Binding	1 yard

Cutting Requirements:

Outside Star Points	8 - 2" Easy Eight™ strips
Inside Star (floral)	16 - 2" Easy Eight™ strips
Inside Star Points	18 - 2" Easy Eight™ strips
Background (large star)	8 - 4½" strips
Counter-cut	48 - Easy Angle II™ triangles
Counter-cut	48 - Easy Angle II™ squares
Background (small star)	7 - 2½" strips
Counter-cut	80 - 2½" squares
Counter-cut	80 - 2½" Easy Angle™ triangles
Small Star Points	8 - 2" Easy Eight™ strips
Sashing	7½" strips

Nora's Star Construction

After cutting the star strips with the Easy Eight™ on the 2" line, sew an outside color to the print; then sew an inside color to the print.

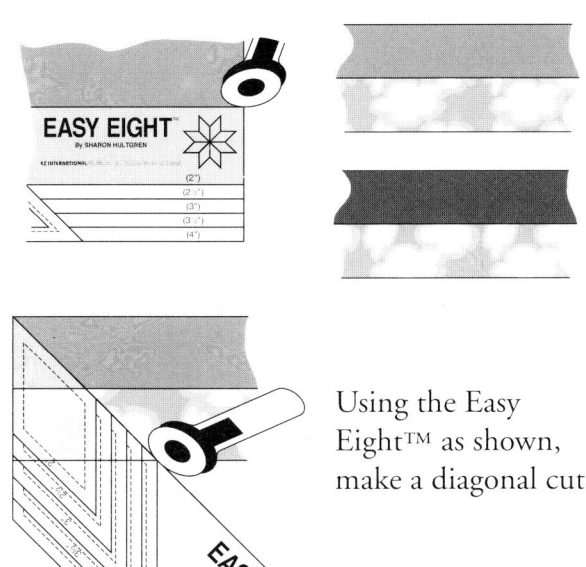

Using the Easy Eight™ as shown, make a diagonal cut.

Continue cutting using the 2" finished edge as the guide. Cut eight pieces from each of the sewn strip sets.

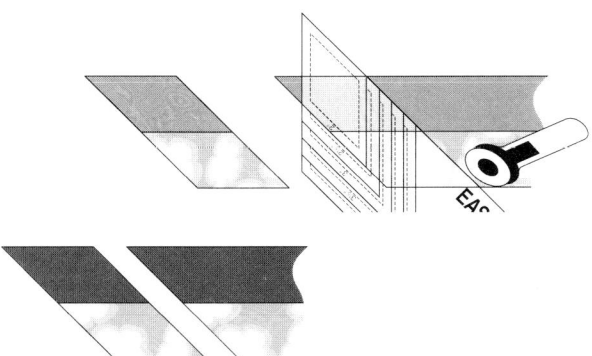

Sew one of each color combination together to form the points of the star. Sew these together first in pairs, then in halves and then complete

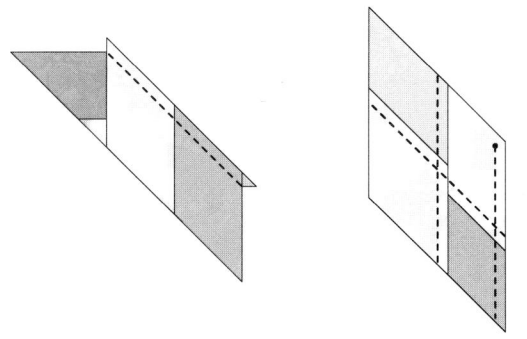

the star. Leave the seam open ¼" on the outside where a square or triangle will be sewn in. You will make twelve stars for this quilt.

Take the Easy Angle II™ squares and triangles and set these into the large star.

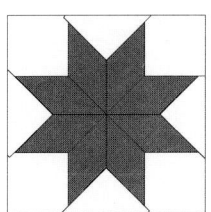

Make twenty of the small stars for the sashing. For each star, piece eight Easy Eight™ diamonds cut from strips using the 2" finished line. Set in the Easy Angle™ squares and triangles.

Measure the small star block from raw edge to raw edge. This will give you the width to cut the sashing strips. (It should be 7¼".) Now measure the side of the large star. (This should be 14".) Cut the sashing pieces by these measurements.

Assemble the quilt as shown. Sew sashing strips to the side of the large stars. Sew sashing strips to the small stars with sashing going the other way. Join these as rows.

Paducah or Flying Bats!
No photo available.

Tools Needed:
Easy Angle™
Easy Angle II™
Easy Eight™

When we go to Paducah to attend the American Quilters Society Quilt Show, one of the things we all look forward to is finding old quilts. This is one I found. The design seemed to have such strength, it seemed like a man's quilt. When I came home, imagine my surprise when I found the block in the book, *Old Patchwork Quilts and The Women Who Make Them* (by Ruth E. Finley, J. B. Lippincott Co., 1929.) Here is what she says, "Flying Bats. Today only men and women lucky enough to spend summer nights in remote woodland camps know the eerie sensation produced by the zigzag dartings of these leather-winged creatures. Bats were once familiar to everyone, and the light of unscreened windows and doors, open to the hot darkness, frequently attracted them inside. Here, blinded by the lamps, they flapped and blundered against wall and ceiling, while the women ducked and screamed and the boys make a great game of chasing the intruders out." Needless to say that after reading this the quilt has a different attraction to me. I know the fabrics are very old as is the pattern, but I prefer to think of it as my Paducah quilt.

Block Construction

Begin by cutting the diamond fabric into strips following the 2½" mark on the Easy Eight™. Sew two strips together and then once again cut on the 2½" mark. Sew two of these pieces together to form the large diamond. From the dark fabric cut a 5½" strip. Cut four triangles and one square. Sew the triangles to the diamond.

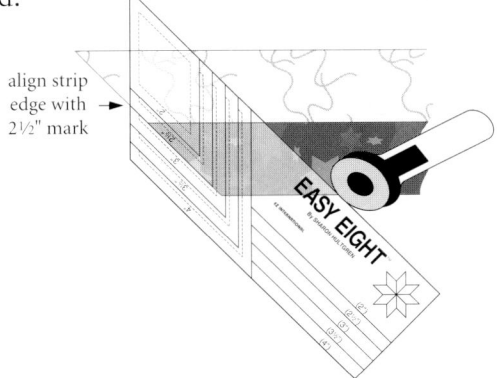

Make four of these units.

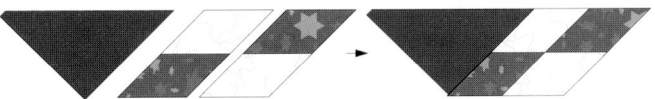

Sew them together in the corners to make a square donut. Set the square into the donut. The block will be 12½" when it is finished. This quilt requires 30 blocks made like this.

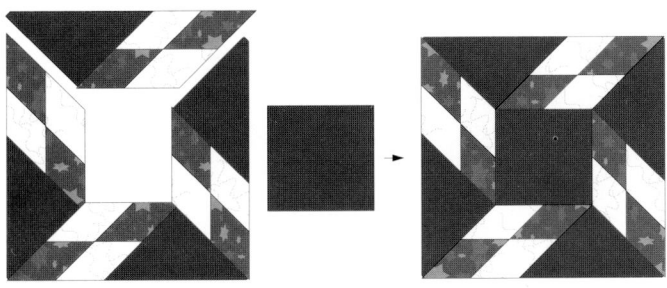

For the background squares cut 7 - 12½" strips. Counter-cut these into 20 - 12½" squares. Cut six 18" squares, then cut these diagonally into quarters. These will be the edge setting triangles.

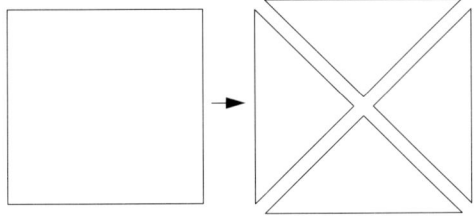

Cut two of the edge setting triangles in half for the corner triangles.

Combine the *Paducah* blocks, the alternating squares and the corner and edge setting triangles as shown below. Sew blocks together in diagonal rows. Sew rows together.

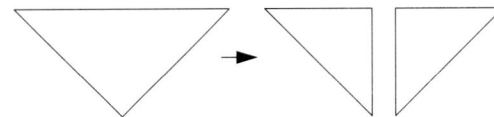

Cut ten 5½" strips for the border. The quilt will measure 91" x 108".

Fabric Requirements:

Diamonds	1½ yds lights
	1½ yds darks
Squares & Triangles	2 yds
Background White	4 yds
Border & Binding	2½ yds

Permission given to copy this page for personal use only.

Permission given to copy this page for personal use only.